WOMEN WORLD LEADERS PRESENTS

Miracle Mindset

FINDING HOPE IN THE CHAOS

VISIONARY AUTHORS

Kelley Rene and Julie T. Jenkins

Miracle Mindset: Finding Hope in the Chaos
Copyright © 2023 Women World Leaders

World Publishing and Productions,
PO Box 8722, Jupiter, FL 33468;
worldpublishingandproductions.com

ISBN: 978-1-957111-16-2

Library of Congress Control Number: 2023916893

Scripture quotations marked AMP are taken from *The Amplified® Bible,* Copyright © 1954, 1958, 1962, 1964, 1965, 1987, by the Lockman Foundation. Used by permission. (www.Lockman.org.) All rights reserved.

Scripture quotations marked ASV are taken from the American Standard Version. Public Domain.

Scripture quotations marked *ESV® Bible are taken from (The Holy Bible, English Standard Version®),* Copyright © 2001 by Crossway, a publishing ministry of Good News Publishers. Used by permission. All rights reserved.

Scripture quotations marked KJV are taken from the King James Version. Public Domain.

Scripture quotations marked MSG are taken from *THE MESSAGE,* copyright © 1993, 2002, 2018 by Eugene H. Peterson. Used by permission of NavPress. All rights reserved. Represented by Tyndale House Publishers, Inc

Scripture quotations marked NASB are taken from the New American Standard Bible®, Copyright ©1960, 1962, 1963, 1968, 1971, 1972, 1973, 1975, 1977, 1995 by the Lockman Foundation. Used by permission.

Scripture quotations marked NIV are taken from THE HOLY BIBLE, NEW INTERNATIONAL VERSION®, NIV® Copyright © 1973, 1978, 1984, 2011 by Biblica, Inc.® Used by permission. All rights reserved worldwide.

Scripture quotations marked NKJV are taken from the New King James Version®. Copyright © 1982 by Thomas Nelson. Used by permission. All rights reserved.

Scripture quotations marked NLT are taken from the *Holy Bible,* New Living Translation, copyright © 1996, 2004, 2015 by Tyndale House Foundation. Used by permission of Tyndale House Publishers, Inc., Carol Stream, Illinois 60188. All rights reserved.

Scripture quotations marked NRSVA are taken from the New Revised Standard Version Bible: Anglicised Edition, copyright © 1989, 1995 the Division of Christian Education of the National Council of the Churches of Christ in the United States of America. Used by permission. All rights reserved.

Scripture quotations marked (TLB) are taken from The Living Bible copyright © 1971. Used by permission of Tyndale House Publishers, Inc., Carol Stream, Illinois 60188. All rights reserved.

Scripture marked (TLV) taken from the Holy Scriptures, Tree of Life Version®. Copyright © 2014,2016 by the Tree of Life Bible Society. Used by permission of the Tree of Life Bible Society.

Scripture quotations marked TPT are from The Passion Translation®. Copyright © 2017, 2018, 2020 by Passion & Fire Ministries, Inc. Used by permission. All rights reserved. ThePassionTranslation.com.

Scripture quotations marked (Voice) are taken from The Voice™. Copyright © 2008 by Ecclesia Bible Society. Used by permission. All rights reserved.

TABLE OF CONTENTS

Introduction vii

About the Cover xiii

Expecting God's Wonder and Awe, Julie T. Jenkins 1

Total Surrender, Kelley Rene 17

Messy Miracles, Connie Ann VanHorn 33

Identity Crisis, DeAnn Alaine 47

Sweet Miracle, Lisa Hathaway 61

Bulldog Faith, Carol Turko 75

Fighting for Nothing, Kat Pennington 89

Greatness Is in You!, Samie V. Maxineau............................ 103

Busting Through the Roof, Ellie McGraw 117

Ordinary Miracles, Leecy Barnett 133

God's Grace and Mercy, One Day at a Time,
Melissa Gissy Witherspoon 147

Who I Think I Am Isn't Who God Says I Am,
Kimberly Ewell 161

Trust the Process, Thayse Edgett Price 177

Divine Providence, Keily J. Denny 191

A Bruised Reed He Will Not Break,
Jane "Goldie" Winn 205

Breathing on Chaos, Diane Lawbaugh 219

Recognizing God Winks to Develop a Miracle Mindset,
Dawn Vazquez 235

Through The Waves, Sarah Bussard 249

The Miracle in Mistakes, Kelly Williams Hale 263

Purple Flowers, Karen Burch 279

INTRODUCTION

It is not an accident that you are holding this book. On the contrary, it's a miracle!

And the more astounding fact is that this is just one of the innumerable miracles God is granting in and through your life today. We often attribute the word "miracle" to something unlikely or surprising, but at its core, a miracle is a work of God. And because God's intricate and awe-inspiring works constantly surround us, we have become desensitized to their presence. That is why we wrote this book. As authors, we chose to band together to tell our stories—stories of God's miracles—as a reminder that we have the privilege of going through life with a Miracle Mindset.

Having a Miracle Mindset is recognizing God's presence even in chaotic moments. One of God's attributes is that He is omnipresent, which means He is always with us. David, as he was dealing with his own chaos, reveled in God's presence, writing: *Where can I go from your Spirit? Where can I flee from your presence? If I go up to the heavens, you are there; if I make my bed in the depths, you are there. If I rise on the wings of the dawn, if I settle on the far side of the sea, even there your hand will guide me, your right hand will hold me fast* (Psalm 139:7-10 NIV).

Those with a Miracle Mindset look for God's glory in the physical realm: the sun that rises in the morning and the stars that shine at night. *The heav-*

ens tell of the glory of God; And their expanse declares the work of His hands (Psalm 19:1 NASB).

And they seek God's awe in the spiritual realm as His hand moves in both celebratory times and difficult circumstances. The Sons of Korah recognized God's works despite standing in the shadow of their ancestor who turned against God. They wrote: *Why are you cast down, O my soul? And why are you disquieted within me? Hope in God; for I shall yet praise him, the help of my countenance and my God* (Psalm 42:11 NKJV).

Clinging to a Miracle Mindset requires intentionally taking our eyes off ourselves and refocusing our attention on our Savior; finding hope through our relationship with God the Father, God the Son, and God the Holy Spirit; and praising Him for His goodness regardless of what we see in the natural. *Oh, give thanks to the Lord! Call upon His name; Make known His deeds among the peoples! Sing to Him, sing psalms to Him; Talk of all His wondrous works! Glory in His holy name; Let the hearts of those who rejoice seek the Lord!* (Psalm 105:1-3 NKJV).

Experiencing life with a Miracle Mindset allows us to uncover God's hidden works in circumstances that may appear dull, tragic, or even superficially exciting, enabling us to explore the depth of His glory.

But harnessing a Miracle Mindset may require a shift in our thinking. A shift from being self-centered to being God-centered. A shift from seeking what we want to relishing what God wants for us. *But as it is written: "Eye has not seen, nor ear heard, nor have entered into the heart of man the things which God has prepared for those who love Him"* (1 Corinthians 2:9 NKJV).

As you read the chapters of this book, you will repeatedly see stories from and references to the Bible. Scripture is not a list of do's and don'ts or a collection of mythical stories from ancient peoples. It is the inspired Word of

God, written so we can know His character. The pages in the Bible convey a love story—God's love for us—and are full of lessons and wisdom for our lives. Learning about God helps us recognize His work and hear His voice. You see, God didn't just speak and perform miracles in days gone by; God is still in the miracle-working business. And one of His greatest miracles is allowing us to know Him.

God longs for us to know Him and fully immerse ourselves in His love for us. He desires to reveal Himself to us, which He does by answering our prayers, responding to our cries for help, and speaking into our spirit. *But those who hope in the Lord will renew their strength. They will soar on wings like eagles; they will run and not grow weary, they will walk and not be faint* (Isaiah 40:31 NIV).

Throughout the Old Testament, men of God built altars to worship and memorialize His incredible works. Abraham and his son Isaac are recorded as doing so. Years later, Jacob would follow suit. *There he built an altar, and he called the place El Bethel, because it was there that God revealed himself to him when he was fleeing from his brother* (Genesis 35:7 NIV). These became holy places to praise God and remember how He moved on their behalf.

Miracle Mindset: Finding Hope in the Chaos is our symbolic altar. We invite you to praise and worship God with us as we memorialize and share the incredible things God has done in our lives. We pray that through our stories, God will open your heart and eyes to the mighty miracles He is orchestrating in your life.

Read each chapter, basking in the revelation that as each author sought after God, He showed up to minister in her life, connect with her, and shine His light in her heart. *We now have this light in our hearts, but we ourselves are like fragile jars containing this great treasure. This makes it clear that our great power is from God, not from ourselves* (2 Corinthians 4:7 NLT).

Then, as you read the teachings, seek God's instructions for your life as you allow Him to shine in and through you. Reach out to Him and take hold of His hand as He creates a Miracle Mindset in you.

May your unfailing love be with us, LORD, even as we put our hope in you (Psalm 33:22 NIV).

ABOUT THE COVER

Prophetic artist Lynne Hudson paints with God, infused by the power of the Holy Spirit. She depends on Him to guide her brush, visually creating what is on His heart. Her original artwork, Celebrate Life, depicted on the cover, illustrates God's desire to release and renew the mindsets of His children. The wave encircling the woman's head represents His anointed cleansing. The butterflies, doves, flowers, and feathers sweeping around her depict the wonders, miracles, and freedom He has in store for us when we set our minds on Him. God longs for us to release our chaos, hoping in Him as He embraces us with His love and surrounds us with His miracles.

And they were all struck with astonishment and began glorifying God...saying, "We have seen remarkable things today!" (Luke 5:26 NASB).

Lynne Hudson lives on the Gold Coast, Australia. Her calling is to help others hear the voice of God through her art. For commissions, art prints, and inquiries, visit www.lynnehudson.com

JULIE T. JENKINS

Julie T. Jenkins is the co-CEO of Women World Leaders and World Publishing and Productions. She loves giving her time and talents to our Lord. Julie is partnered with Kimberly Hobbs to oversee WWL as she guides the ministry coordinators, writes for and leads the editing team of *Voice of Truth* magazine, and hosts "Walking in the Word"—the weekly biblical teaching episode of the *Women World Leaders' Podcast.* Additionally, she is a Bible teacher and best-selling author. Through WPP, Julie is honored to serve as a writing coach and editor for those called to share their God-story with the world.

Born in Indiana and raised in Ohio, Julie earned her Bachelor of Communications from The University of Tulsa and her Master's of Biblical Exposition from Moody Bible College. She traveled in Up With People, was a long-time Bible Study Fellowship leader and teacher, and has completed multiple biblical and leadership training programs.

Julie and her husband, Michael, have been married for 27 years, live in Jupiter, Florida, and own and operate J29 Marketing—a full-service digital marketing company. They have three children of whom they are immensely proud.

Julie can be contacted at julie@womenworldleaders.com or julie@worldpublishingandproductions.com

Expecting God's Wonder and Awe

by Julie T. Jenkins

When I was a child, I remember crawling into a cave with my parents and siblings for a family adventure. It was dark. The tunnel through the rocks was so narrow we had to slither on our bellies. The surroundings were unfamiliar. And I didn't really know where we were going. But I did know that as long as I followed my dad closely, I would be okay.

Eventually, we made our way into a much larger opening—the heart of the cave—where I could see beautiful rock formations extending in the distance. As I stood up, holding my father's hand, I marveled at both what we had been through and God's miraculous display now before us.

Going through life can be like sliding through the darkness of a cave on your belly. We proceed down narrow passages, trusting the One leading us, and emerge to an unexpectedly glorious view. One of the longest and most rewarding adventures of my life is the one called parenting. Through it, I have learned that when we allow God to guide us down unfamiliar paths that are sometimes dark and uncertain, He will not only lead us to a breathtaking view, but He will also reveal the wonder and awe of His miracles along the way.

THE MIRACLE OF PROTECTION

It was an ordinary afternoon at the ice skating rink. My oldest daughter, Sarah, had fallen in love with the sport, so we—my three children and I—regularly spent many hours in one of the coldest buildings in Tampa, Florida.

Sarah was a lively and talented 7-year-old with a dazzling smile who strived to excel in everything she did. Emily, my second-born, was five. With her white blonde hair, light pink lips, and piercing blue eyes, she was already determined to make her own way in the world and had no problem finding creative ways to keep herself occupied while her sister was busy on the ice. My youngest, Matthew, was just one. He didn't speak much—the doctor said he didn't have to because his sisters spoke for him—but his gaze was captivating when his big blue eyes would lock with yours.

Matthew and I were sitting high up on the permanent wooden bleachers. It was a fun place for him to explore as he crawled back and forth the five feet or so between me and the constructed wall at the end. The solid wooden benches that reached high up into the arena were uncomfortable, but they were sturdy and stable and offered a good view of the ice. Occasionally, Matthew would pull himself up to a standing position, reminding me it wouldn't be long before this location would no longer be a safe place for my soon-to-be-toddler to toddle in.

It had been a tough season. My husband, Michael, had taken a new job in Ohio. Trying hard not to disrupt the children's schooling, I stayed behind with the kids as they finished out their year. Adding to our burden, my dad, who lived an hour from us, had been diagnosed with an inoperable brain tumor about five months earlier. He had spent a few months undergoing treatments near our home in Tampa before entering hospice care near his own home, where he died peacefully. I had been doing my best to care for my children and emotionally support my parents for months. Graciously, God had put in place people and provisions to see me through—most notably my neighbor, who helped immensely with the kids.

As I sat at the rink, keeping an eye on all three children, Matthew crawled, once again, to the end of the row, pulled himself up to a standing position, and then plopped back on his bottom, his eyes locking with mine as he grinned. Then, with laughter, he leaned back against the solid wall at the end of the bleachers. And then he was gone.

The "wall" I'd always thought was solid suddenly revealed itself to be heavy fabric that allowed my son to slip through and fall 15 feet to the cement floor beneath.

Gasping, I flew down the bleachers and found my boy lying on the cement floor. His eyes were wide as he stared up at me. Without thinking, I grabbed him and called for his sisters, my voice echoing through the rink that we had to leave—"Now!" Shaking, we ran to the car. I called my mom, and she said she would meet us at the hospital. Then I called my neighbor and told her I needed to drop off the girls.

I arrived at the hospital and rushed in with Matthew in my arms. He still hadn't made a sound. I told the emergency room attendant that he had fallen 15 feet to a cement floor. She looked at me in disbelief. "Fifteen feet? He looks fine."

"I know. Yes. Fifteen feet." It was all I could do to breathe.

The emergency room was packed. After completing the appropriate paperwork, we were instructed to have a seat until we were called. My mom arrived, and we continued to wait among people who were visibly sick. In time, Matthew climbed down from my lap and began a fun game of pushing an empty chair around the waiting room.

I watched his joyful presence and began to process all that had occurred, realizing I was face-to-face with a miracle. Against all odds, my boy was okay. God had protected him. With my mom's guidance, I squelched all the rational thoughts in my head about what should have been happening in Matthew's body after such a fall and, with a Miracle Mindset, leaned into the wonder before me.

THE MIRACLE OF GOD'S PRESENCE

If I've said it once, I've said it a thousand times: I don't know how anyone gets through life without turning to Jesus. And I certainly don't know how parents get through parenting without relying on God.

The prophet Isaiah said, *"Woe to the obstinate children," declares the Lord, "to those who carry out plans that are not mine"* (Isaiah 30:1 NIV). Isaiah was prophesying God's words to the people of Judah. It was a difficult time for God's people, and yet they made things worse for themselves by rebelling against God and rejecting His message. The Lord told them, *"In repentance and rest is your salvation, in quietness and trust is your strength"* (Isaiah 30:15 NIV), but they would have none of it. Instead, they sought wisdom and protection from a worldly source.

As God's children, we can trust Him with our every step, seeking His wisdom and guidance and expecting His miracles. God promises us so much. As Isaiah proclaimed to the people of Judah, *The Lord longs to be gracious to you; therefore he will rise up to show you compassion...Blessed are all who wait for him!* (Isaiah 30:18 NIV). What a comfort that should be to us!

Our oldest was born on March 11, 2000. And God showed up right away. Before her grand arrival into the world, Sarah had gotten tangled in her umbilical cord and was being strangled with each contraction. The phenomenal medical staff performed an emergency cesarean section, then whisked our blue baby off to receive special treatment. Before the delivery, my husband and I decided that if anything should go wrong, he would go with our daughter to support and love her. We did not want her to be alone. This left me alone on the operating table, but not really. Sarah recovered quickly, but the more impressionable miracle was that God never left any of us alone. He was with me on that operating table, and He was also with my husband and our newborn. God's miraculous presence is astounding.

When Emily was born two years later, I came face-to-face with a fear of how our little family of three would change. I went into labor early, and when I realized there was no turning back, I broke out in tears, full of questions and trepidation. But God was there, and He spoke through my husband, encouraging me to press on, that God was in control.

And hours before our youngest was born, a different fear gripped me. Although my pregnancy had gone well, suddenly, I was hit with a paralyzing thought: *What if something is wrong with my son? Am I prepared?*

Let's face it. Parenting is its own kind of chaos. Parenting dredges up heightened emotions and complicated thoughts as we give life to and then, slowly but surely, lose control of the little humans we have been given the privilege of caring for.

But God promises He will never leave us alone. That is a miracle worth holding on to!

THE MIRACLE OF GROWTH

He will also send you rain for the seed you sow in the ground, and the food that comes from the land will be rich and plentiful (Isaiah 30:23 NIV).

Growing is not easy—and as parents, our calling is to help our children grow even as we mature. As my children have gone through different phases of life, I've turned to God many times with the simple prayer: *God, I don't know how to do this. Give me your wisdom. Help me be a good parent.* And He has always responded—often teaching me through the care and words of others.

Each of you should use whatever gift you have received to serve others, as faithful stewards of God's grace in its various forms (1 Peter 4:10 NIV).

From my daughter's second-grade teacher, I learned to expect that God's miracles in my children's lives would exceed my own expectations, "The careers these children will have are not even in existence yet. My job is to teach them how to think and learn."

I learned to witness the miracle of guided brain development from another teacher who taught me, "It's okay to let your daughter struggle, but always let her know you are there. When she is doing her homework, do something you enjoy, but be present in case she needs you."

Over and over, I learned not to stifle God's miraculous plans, allowing each child to flourish in his own gifting. A preschool teacher was among the first to see my daughter's leadership strengths and encourage her to develop them. A Girl Scout leader taught me my child would thrive if I let her exercise her independence, even when that meant I felt less relevant for a time. And coach after coach helped me learn to expect the unexpected—because my kids were tougher, more resilient, and gifted in more areas than I could ever imagine.

Allowing our kids to grow isn't always easy, and trusting others to guide them can be downright scary. But when we walk with God in obedience, trusting His leading, He will surprise us.

As a parent, I prayed over and over: *God, I don't know how to do this. Give me your wisdom. Help me be a good parent.*

And God sent His people to aid in the miracle of growth that my children—and I—needed.

THE MIRACLE OF PROVISION

Like all families, ours has had its share of ups and downs, good days and bad days. There have been times of financial plenty and seasons when the field seemed barren. Sometimes everything works like clockwork, while at other points, it has felt like nothing would ever go right again. And there have been moments of peace and joy and days when I've wanted to scream, "Can't we all just get along?!"

But through it all, having a Miracle Mindset has helped me remember that God is always in control. He simply asks us to lean on Him and do the next right thing.

We've gone on a variety of vacations as a family. All have been partially successful! Some of our favorite getaways have been when we've rented a home in the mountains a day's drive away.

On one such trip, as we were driving back from a day of hiking, one daughter started crying that her eye hurt and her contact was stuck. We pulled over to examine her eye, but I could not see the contact in it anywhere. Eventually, my daughter calmed down enough to recognize that the pain had subsided. We surmised that the contact had to be in the van somewhere—in the van that was loaded down with five people and a mess of snacks and smelly hiking gear. So we all searched...and searched...and searched for the missing contact. Finally, we had no choice but to give up the search and continue back to the house.

The ride was quiet. We were all frustrated. In my mind, I prayed that God would guide us and let this all work out. Yet as we drove, trying to de-escalate the situation for my daughter, whose sight without lenses is so bad that she has a difficult time getting around, the news seemed to get more and more disheartening.

"When we get back to the house, you can just put in a new contact. You brought a spare pair, right?"

"No."

Silence.

"Well, I guess you'll just have to wear your glasses for the rest of the trip."

"I didn't bring them."

Oh, how I wanted to scream, but what was the use?

We had scheduled and pre-paid for a river rafting trip for the next morning. We were all excited as this was something we had unanimously enjoyed in the past—which is saying something with five very different personalities. But the outing would be next-to-impossible if my daughter could not see.

We returned to the house and cooked our pre-planned spaghetti dinner, all while each trying to troubleshoot the situation. Boil the noodles. *Do you know your prescription?* Brown the meat. *Could we contact her eye doctor?* Cut the onions, mushrooms, and peppers. *Is there an optometrist nearby?* Prepare the garlic bread. *Maybe someone should check the van again.*

But it was the weekend. We were in the middle of nowhere. Cell service was spotty. And it had now been several hours since the contact went missing—even if we DID find it, it would certainly be dried out.

We ate dinner, resigned that this simple issue could derail our getaway. All of us trying not to be angry. All of us trying to let God guide our thoughts and words.

After dinner, I began washing the dishes. I reached to pick up the colander, and as I was about to place it in the soapy water, I noticed a piece of plastic stuck to the bottom. With two fingers, I picked up the object in awe. Surely it couldn't be. But it was! The contact! How in the world did it end up in the colander?

I called to my daughter, who quickly grabbed her contact solution, cleaned the contact, and put it in her eye as we all watched expectantly. It had to be ruined. But, no. It was perfect.

Oh, there are SO many times in our parenting journey when God has provided in miraculous ways! And some have been far more impactful for the long term than a lost contact on a vacation. God has provided financially, placed us in the right neighborhoods and school districts, and given us amazing church families, employment opportunities, and wisdom for difficult decisions. But what I love most about this miracle—and it was indeed a miracle—is that God provided something that we didn't need; instead, His provision enabled us to enjoy each other's presence and the beauty of His nature as we sought a season of rest.

God showed us, through that one contact, that He loves us so much that He will take care of even the little things. His provision is always perfect. And that is miraculous.

THE MIRACLE OF GOD'S LOVE AND POWER

My kids are getting older now. They are 23, 21, and 17, and we are in the phase of "letting go."

As I look back, it is astounding to see how God has increased my faith in Him as I've traveled this path of parenting. I've learned to be grateful for His ever-present protection, begun to realize with awe that He is always with me, marveled at the growth He has orchestrated in all our lives, and sat in wonder at how He has continually provided through thick and thin.

Now, as my children strike out on their own, God is teaching me of His all-consuming love and His unfathomable power. With an intentional Miracle Mindset, I can step back and watch Him care for my adult children. I can trust the love and power He is constantly pouring into their lives as I release them fully into His hands, witnessing with wonder and awe their continued transformation into all He has called them to be.

Parenting is chaotic. And sometimes, the path is dark. But God's love and power abound, lighting the way and leading us to a miraculous view. And as we continue to make our way through the tunnels of life, we are blessed to remember that His miracles always surround us.

- He protects us. *"So do not fear, for I am with you; do not be dismayed, for I am your God. I will strengthen you and help you; I will uphold you with my righteous right hand"* (Isaiah 41:10 NIV).

- He never leaves us. *"The Lord himself goes before you and will be with you; he will never leave you nor forsake you"* (Deuteronomy 31:8 NIV).

- He ensures our growth. *The righteous will flourish like a palm tree, they will grow like a cedar of Lebanon* (Psalm 92:12 NIV).

- His provision is sure. *Do not set your heart on what you will eat or drink; do not worry about it. For the pagan world runs after all such things, and your Father knows that you need them. But seek his kingdom, and these things will be given to you as well* (Luke 12:29-31 NIV).

- And His inexhaustible love and power are always present. *For I am convinced that neither death nor life, neither angels nor demons, neither the present nor the future, nor any powers, neither height nor depth, nor anything else in all creation, will be able to separate us from the love of God that is in Christ Jesus our Lord* (Romans 8:38-39 NIV).

The gift of parenting is one that lasts forever. Holding on to a Miracle Mindset down the sometimes dark and winding path allows us to bask in His awesome wonders available to us at every turn.

As you walk, or even slide on your belly, through the chaos of life, keep your mind set on God's miracles all around you. They are there, even in the darkness. And when the tunnel opens up to a majestic view, grab your Father's hand and stand up tall—knowing He has been with you all along.

FINDING THE MIRACLE IN OUR STRUGGLES

by Kelley Rene

Moses experienced them. David experienced them. We certainly all would agree that Job experienced them. And we can also add Peter to the mix.

What do these men of the Bible have in common?

They each struggled against unwarranted circumstances and personal inadequacies. But they also have something more significant in common: their struggles weren't the end of their stories.

Moses, struggling against low self-esteem and a lack of self-confidence, ran into the desert when God appeared to him in a burning bush. But ultimately, he obeyed God and successfully led the Israelites out of bondage. At first, the people sang and danced praises to God. But their jubilation was short-lived as they soon discovered there was no water in the desert for them to drink. Moses responded by harnessing God's power. *Then the people complained and turned against Moses. "What are we going to drink?" they demanded. So Moses cried out to the Lord for help, and the Lord showed him a piece of wood. Moses threw it into the water, and this made the water good to drink* (Exodus 15:24-25 NLT).

David, the anointed king of Israel, struggled for his life against a madman, King Saul, who hunted him for many years. Although David's life was in danger, and he grew weary of living in caves and hiding from his enemies, he held fast to God as he wrote in Psalm 142:1-2, *I cry out to the Lord; I plead for the Lord's mercy. I pour out my complaints before him and tell him all my troubles* (NLT).

Job was a wealthy man who struggled against tragedy after tragedy, including losing his children, animals, crops, and even his health. But although he faced inner torment in his calamity, Job refused to curse God. *Job stood up and tore his robe in grief. Then he shaved his head and fell to the ground to worship. He said, "I came naked from my mother's womb, and I will be naked when I leave. The Lord gave me what I had, and the Lord has taken it away. Praise the name of the Lord!"* (Job 1:20-21 NLT).

And Peter, as recorded in Mark 14:27-31, struggled against fear, which led him to deny Christ three times, just as Jesus predicted. He then returned to his life as a fisherman, facing defeat and discouragement. But just a few days later, when Jesus appeared on the shore while Peter was fishing, Peter immediately jumped into the water and swam to greet Him (John 21).

Despite their struggles and failures, each of these men ultimately responded to God. With humility. With worship. And God received them and ministered to their needs.

He desires to do the same for us.

Is life pulling you in a direction you don't want to go? Is God calling you to do something that you're resisting? Are you tired and worn out from struggling with those things that don't make sense in your life?

Turn and run toward God! He is more than able to align your heart with His and *cause everything to work together for your good* (Romans 8:28 NLT).

Dear brothers and sisters, when troubles of any kind come your way, consider it an opportunity for great joy. For you know that when your faith is tested, your endurance has a chance to grow. So let it grow, for when your endurance is fully developed, you will be perfect and complete, needing nothing (James 1:2-4 NLT).

To find the miracle in our struggles, we must humble ourselves before God and cry out to Him. He can and will infuse hope into our chaos and bring us peace.

. . . .

KELLEY RENE

Kelley Rene is an award-winning author who resides in Panama City Beach, Florida, with her husband and mini Australian Shepherd, Blossom. She loves to meet new people and experience new places, often the inspiration for her stories. She desires to be a conduit of God's love and forgiveness.

Kelley serves as president of PROTalkers, a virtual Toastmasters International club, and Chair for the District 25 Speakers Bureau. She prides herself in helping others overcome the fear of public speaking and gain confidence in their calling. Kelley recently launched Palm Branch Publishing to aid fiction writers towards publication. Its inaugural book will release in 2024.

As a Women World Leader, she is a regular contributor in the magazine *Voice of Truth,* with her column *Through The Eyes Of Merci.* She also contributed in the #1 Amazon Bestseller Embrace the Journey, collaborated on *Next Chapters Unleashed (2022 BookFest Winner),* and self-published three novellas, *Saving Sabine (2022 BookFest Winner), Romanian Runaway (2022 BookFest Winner),* and *Kamilah.*

When she's not scribbling out fiction, you'll find her crocheting, kayaking, enjoying the beach, or cuddling a good book and cappuccino. Keep up with her at kelleyrene.com or on Goodreads, Facebook, and Instagram @imkelleyrene.

TOTAL SURRENDER

by Kelley Rene

Not my will, but Yours be done, Father.

It is a simple prayer I'd learned from my mother—a prayer that would become the standard for my life. One that would get me through many difficult days and remind me to give God the glory in all things.

"Don't you think he deserves to know?" Reverend Miracle's eyes bore into mine from across the large oak desk cluttered with Bibles and reference books. "If you suspect you can't conceive, that's something the two of you should know before you get married. Don't you think?"

Up to that point, our required premarital counseling had gone well. Both of us, juniors in college, talked openly and honestly about our future, each eager to start our marriage right. I swallowed hard, feeling exposed and ashamed. I stammered in the affirmative. Beside me, my fiancé was quiet. When questioned, he nodded in agreement. He grew up an only child. I knew he wanted a family.

The next week, I followed our minister's advice and visited a gynecologist to discover the reason I very rarely experienced a menstrual cycle.

"I honestly can't explain it. We've done every test imaginable." Dr. Henley wrung her hands as if to free herself of the confusion spread across her face.

"It will be a miracle if you ever get pregnant."

Although I had suspected as much, shock and horror gripped me.

The doctor's words stayed with me, and I've quoted her many times through the years. The first occurred when I delivered the news to my fiancé with tears streaming down my face. To my complete relief, he didn't see it as a reason to call off our wedding.

However, in less than two years, we experienced our miracle. We were expecting.

Initially, I was too surprised and excited to foresee how this new development would impact my life plans which were all spelled out in black and white on notebook paper. Obtain my accounting degree. Work my way up to executive of an accounting firm. Buy a custom BMW. The list clearly outlined my life goals. I left nothing out. Everything I ever dreamed of accomplishing was included. And one by one, I intended to check them off.

Our excitement grew faster than my belly, but eventually, our coming addition was obvious.

Then it started. The stares and glares. The looks of disapproval. I hadn't considered how it would look. Me. A college girl. On campus. Pregnant.

All of a sudden, being pregnant felt like the plague. I jokingly considered wearing a billboard over my midsection that read: It's okay. I'm married. But the reality was, it wasn't okay. Being pregnant went against the exploding feminist movement sweeping across college campuses. I felt such scorn I began to avoid going to campus at all costs. This was before Zoom, teleconferencing, and hybrid meetings. My grades suffered.

One day, I stepped onto the elevator after a deflating meeting with my guidance counselor. Just before the doors closed, in stepped one of my professors, who I greatly admired. He was starchy in personality but thorough and generous with his explanations in class, especially with those of us who asked a lot of questions. I smiled and greeted him.

"Why are you still here?" His stoic nature was normal, and I replied simply that I had a meeting.

He motioned toward my bulging stomach. "No, I mean, why are you still here? In school?"

The insult in his words birthed a defiance in me that plumed in my gut and formed the words that came out of my mouth. "Because I've worked very hard, and I have every intention of completing my degree."

His face showed disdain as he stepped off the elevator, leaving me stunned and demoralized.

The warrior woman in me—or maybe it was my maternal instincts kicking in early—postured for a fight. Having a baby was beautiful. Having a baby was natural. Having a baby was a miracle. My miracle! I would not cower. I would not be embarrassed. I would not quit.

I had already earned my Associate's Degree and was close to completing my Bachelor's Degree. I'd spent a lot of time and energy studying. I'd spent too much money—albeit in the form of student loans—to give up on this dream now. But as often occurs during challenging times, even my family hinted I should drop out of school.

But something in me rebelled. I wouldn't do it. I would finish school. I would attain my degree. I would have my career. And I kept trudging toward the finish line. Even if with less vigor.

The scrutiny I felt prompted comfort eating, which prompted weight gain, which prompted frustration and even depression. All my energy went into my studies, maintaining my part-time job, growing a baby, and holding my head high amongst what felt like many naysayers.

Exhaustion weighed me down. And my grades continued to flounder. Giving up looked better every day.

Our bouncy baby girl arrived two weeks late, but perfectly on time. She was born the Wednesday before spring break, giving us an entire week to enjoy introducing her to family and friends before returning to class.

My husband and I had prepared for this. We'd masterfully crafted our schedules to allow one of us to always be home with our newborn. I wouldn't go back to work for weeks.

But as often happens, life threw a wrench into our plans.

Early in the wee hours Monday morning, as spring break officially ended, I awoke writhing in pain. I made it out of bed only to land on the floor, piercing shards of lightning pain sliced through my midsection. I couldn't speak or call for help. My husband woke to the cries of the baby and found me in the fetal position sobbing next to the crib.

A whirlwind of events ensued: the emergency room, doctor visits, and surgery. All my priorities shifted and took a backseat to my health crisis. Why would God give me a miracle baby but not allow me to live to see her grow? It didn't make sense.

My surgery was successful, but I missed more classes than intended. When I returned, my professors made no allowances for my missed coursework.

I would have to work extra hard to ensure I passed that semester. My GPA took a huge hit.

My sisters visited to help with the baby when I returned to work. But even their assistance couldn't keep me from being distracted by the cries of my colicky infant as I tried to study each evening. All I wanted to do was cuddle her. Console her. Often I'd rock her for hours only to start my homework after midnight. Many times I cried alongside her, exhausted. My drive and determination were surmounted by the pressure and stress in my life.

Some time later, during a meeting with the dean, he offered me a scholarship that allowed me to quit my part-time job. I'd have more time to study. And sleep. That fueled me.

But the daily grind of balancing motherhood with student life took its toll. I lived in two different worlds that did not align. I took one day at a time, knowing that was all I could handle.

And then the inconceivable happened.

I was pregnant. Again. Another miracle baby. *How could this be?*

"It will be a miracle if you ever get pregnant." That's what she'd said. I heard it with my own two ears.

My husband and I celebrated. We managed one. We would manage a second.

God had given us another miracle. He would make a way where there seemed to be no way.

So I trudged on—putting one foot in front of the other. Focused. Determined. Unwavering.

Life was hard. Money was tight. My senior-level coursework seemed impossible, and I was now carrying the weight of a bowling ball in my belly, along with a heavy backpack full of thick textbooks on my back. Our friend group had shifted to two other couples traveling a similar journey. What a blessing they were during those very lonely and challenging days.

That semester was demanding. Graduation was pushed to the fall, and I enrolled in summer classes.

One night, I sat alone in a student area on campus surrounded by well-worn notebooks and study guides. Streetlights streamed into the dimly lit space. My toes throbbed in my binding shoes, but I couldn't reach my swollen feet to provide the needed relief. My back and legs ached. No matter how I twisted, I could not get comfortable. I knew one thing for certain. My future no longer looked the way I'd planned.

"Lord, I refuse to see this pregnancy as a bad thing. I know this baby is a gift from You. Our miracle." Tears spilled down my cheeks. "God. I've spent so much time. So much energy. So much money trying to finish my degree. I've smiled at the opposition, responding in kindness at all the negative comments."

Several students bounced past me with more enthusiasm than should be allowed at midnight. I swiped my wet jaw against a sleeve, hoping no one noticed. "Heavenly Father, please help me accomplish this goal. Everyone expects me to give up, but I don't want to." I shifted, another attempt to relieve the pain screaming in my lower back. "God, if you help me finish, I'll do whatever You call me to do. I want Your will for my life, whatever that looks like. Even if it means I never accomplish another one of my goals."

Fervency I'd never experienced came over me. I could do this. With God's help, I *would* do this.

I can still feel the relief of the day my degree requirements were successfully completed. I had done it! But not without God's ever-present, supernatural help. What I didn't yet realize was the lesson He was teaching me. The phenomenon of seeing and experiencing His presence at work around me: a Miracle Mindset.

The day before my husband and I expected to walk across the stage to receive our diplomas, we stood in the campus bookstore picking through pre-packaged caps and gowns, searching for our sizes. I massaged the pressure squeezing my oversized belly. Not fully grasping I was in labor, I teased him, "We may not make it to graduation."

In a flash, he had me in the car. The hospital was a forty-five-minute climb through the mountains, and he wasn't taking any chances. When we arrived, an ongoing renovation of the building forced him to drop me off at the curb.

I waddled into the hospital, not stopping to check in at the reception or bother with a wheelchair. Inside the elevator, I doubled over, no longer able to breathe through the contractions. A janitor rushed to my aide, and several nurses came running at his calls for help.

The doctor dashed into the delivery room minutes before our second baby—a boy this time—crowned, just forty-five minutes after my arrival at the hospital. He was lodged in the birth canal, and, with a nurse on each side of me, my doctor finessed, finagled, and literally pulled the child out. I watched in horror as the doctor held the newborn upside down against his forearm and pumped the baby's lifeless body against his own thigh. Bam. Bam. Bam. When our baby boy finally squealed, a collective sigh of relief filled the room, and we cried tears of joy. God performed yet another miracle that night.

Several months later, my husband and I received our diplomas in the mail. God had answered my prayer, and I had every intention of keeping my promise of using my life for His glory.

Our third miracle baby arrived two years later, and at that point, we decided to round out our family to an even number. Four babies. Our family would be complete. We spent three years trying for baby number four. Then resigned ourselves to be content with the children God had blessed us with. Life went on.

That is until I recognized the old familiar uneasiness of first-trimester symptoms four years later. I had tossed all my maternity clothes and given away all our baby stuff. We were done. But God clearly had other plans.

We enjoyed celebrating baby number four with our older children, who were excited to have a baby sister. Then two years later—surprise, surprise. Baby number five was on his way.

God gave us five miracle babies. All completely unplanned. By our standards, anyway. We grew accustomed to the typical comments about having a large family and a schedule that was always hectic, busy, and chaotic. My life looked different than I ever imagined. Complete with a mini-van and nonstop shuttle service to all the kids' extracurriculars.

Years later, my mother phoned to tell me she'd found a notebook of mine on which I'd scribbled in black ink a list of my life goals. We laughed as she read it aloud. *Never, ever become a stay-at-home mom* was near the top. Yes, my plan looked very different than God's, but my life was so much richer, living it His Way.

God opened the door for us to live and travel in Europe, and in every place we moved through the years, He gave me opportunities to serve others through my talents and skills, whether in a volunteer capacity or through a paid job. I never regretted letting go of my expectations. My life was in the hands of a master planner. Despite the ebb and flow of life's struggles and challenges, I always trusted God to lead and guide us. And time after time, when details fell into place, I knew we were exactly where we were supposed to be—in His will.

And yet. I often marveled over how things transpired during those early years of our marriage. I could see God's handwriting all over the details. But why? Even in my appreciation, I couldn't comprehend why the God of the Universe would seemingly care so much about my life. My prayers. My family.

Recently, while praying through this chapter for *Miracle Mindset*, I began to ask God. *Who am I, Lord, that You would give me five miracles that I hadn't even asked for?* Weeks later, as I listened to a sermon, the pastor shared about an Easter service where he prayed over an infertile couple desiring to become pregnant.

My earlier question burned in my mind. *God, I never thought to ask for children. The doctor's words were so definitive. Despite my disappointment at the time, we moved on, never mentioning or considering the possibility again. How is it that You would give us children when others desperately desire a child and don't receive their miracle?*

The pastor went on to tell how the couple attended services the following Easter to dedicate their newborn to the Lord. God had answered their prayers.

In that moment, a memory from my early teen years came to me. I was sad, lonely, and confused. Twelve-year-old, innocent Kelley sat on her bed crying and pouring her heart out to God. "Please, God, watch over me.

Be with me all my life. No matter what dumb decisions I make when I get older, please always stay with me. Bless me. Keep me safe and guide all that I do. I want Your will for my life."

As I sat there mesmerized by the scene in my mind, vividly remembering the pain of that day, God whispered into my heart, *I heard your prayers and answered them. I've been with you all along.*

That memory brings tears to my eyes. God had been with me all along. He heard my innocent, desperate prayer and guided me through many tumultuous days.

Our God is a god of miracles. Looking back, having a Miracle Mindset meant surrendering my will to Him. *"For I know the plans I have for you," declares the Lord, "plans to prosper you and not to harm you, plans to give you hope and a future"* (Jeremiah 29:11 NIV). There were so many goals I'd set for myself, but I wanted God's will more. I can see how even from my early days, God was teaching me to have a Miracle Mindset: to keep my attention on Him no matter my circumstances.

A Miracle Mindset tunes our eyes and ears toward God. To have a heart of worship. To have a heart of obedience. To have a heart of love, joy, and peace. To walk out every single day with a heart open to what He is speaking and where He is leading.

God desires to have an authentic relationship with you. Ask Him to give you a mindset that searches for Him everywhere—a laser-sharp focus on what He's doing all around you—and see if He doesn't give you a new revelation. A fresh perspective of His love for you and the purpose He has for your life.

For the Lord your God is living among you. He is a mighty savior. He will take delight in you with gladness. With his love, he will calm all your fears. He will rejoice over you with joyful songs (Zephaniah 3:17 NLT).

The Miracle of the Every Day

by Julie T. Jenkins

On this side of heaven, it is easy to fall into a rut of daily existence: Get up in the morning. Go to work. Care for your family. Go to bed. Then start all over again. But as we work to develop a Miracle Mindset, we will begin to see wonders around us that are so remarkable.

When my three kids were in middle and elementary school, they all attended different schools—necessitating my trek through car line six times a day. Talk about a rut! I worked to be creative with my time, however, and one day, I sat waiting in my car with my engine turned off, windows down, and soaking in the poetry of Genesis. As I read, I marveled at how God created the world, pausing to look up and ponder the miracle of the tree I saw through the front windshield. Taking in the beauty of its bright green leaves, creating much-appreciated shade on that bright Florida day, I thanked God for the miracle of His creation. He truly thought of everything! He gave us the rhythm of the sun and the moon that matches our need for activity and rest; He gave us shade for those times when the sun shines too brightly; AND He made that shade both beautiful and life-giving as the green leaves emit oxygen into the atmosphere.

As I quietly praised God for His goodness, my gaze shifted to the sidewalk, where I saw my daughter walking towards the car, and I audibly gasped. My daughter—what a miracle!

So God created human beings in his own image.
In the image of God he created them;
male and female he created them (Genesis 1:27 NLT).

The truth is, no matter where we look in this world, when we open our eyes with our minds set on seeing the miraculous, we will become witnesses to the incredible wonders all around us! Try it—you just might get a new appreciation for:

- The intricate functions of the cells in our bodies as they work together to keep us alive

- The passage of time, coupled with the wonder of our brains, allowing us to learn and grow

- Feelings and emotions that make us uniquely human

- The awesome phenomenon of the seashore and the glory of the mountaintop

- The intricate and delicate construction of a grain of sand or a falling snowflake

- The sound of a bird at dawn or the violin as it is caressed by the expert musician

- The laugh of a child and the twinkle in her eye as she tastes her favorite ice cream

- The cloud-like softness of a pillow after a long day

These are all miracles created just for you by our miracle-working God.

And there are so many more!

This world is SO packed with God's astonishing miracles that, if we aren't careful, our senses may become dulled to them. Please don't ever let that happen! When the daily grind threatens to take your wonder away, pause. Breathe. And look around with reverence and awe at the every day. Thank God for His goodness as you melt into a mindset intent on seeing the miraculous.

. . . .

CONNIE ANN VANHORN

Connie Ann VanHorn is an ambassador and best-selling author for Women World Leaders. She serves on the Leadership Team and is an ongoing featured writer for *Voice of Truth* magazine. Connie has a heart for encouraging all people to find their God-given purpose.

Connie is an ordinary person whom God spared and gave new life. She is passionate about sharing her story in hopes that God will use it to change lives. Connie wants the whole world to know about her amazing and loving God. She understands that we are all called to share in the same mission.

Connie resides in Winston-Salem, North Carolina, where she has participated in several discipleship classes and taught Sunday school to international students. She has also attended Bible classes at Vintage Bible College.

Being a mother is Connie's greatest accomplishment and her first, best ministry. She dreams of changing the world by sharing Jesus and raising world-changers who have a kingdom perspective.

She enjoys being active in her community, making bracelets, journaling, and spending most of her time with her family. Connie wants her readers to know that it's ok to be broken—it's in our broken place that we find God. See past messy, see past broken, and you might just see a miracle.

MESSY MIRACLES

by Connie Ann VanHorn

I've been walking with God for nine miraculous years. But nine years later, I can testify that my race is not easy. And it surely doesn't look like perfection. Some days are pretty, and some are not. Some days look holy, and others do not. If you are where I am, I want to encourage you to persevere. Don't give up. Keep chasing God. Keep moving those mountains. Have bold FAITH and believe that God can and will do the impossible—even when everything seems messy.

The Bible says if you have faith the size of a mustard seed, you can move mountains. I always wondered what that meant—"move mountains." Was it referring to the mountain-sized stack of bills on the table? I wanted to believe so badly in God's miracle but couldn't wrap my mind around it. Sometimes things are so big and so great that keeping the faith is far beyond our imagination. Even before I was saved, I wanted to believe in something I couldn't see with my own eyes. My life was out of my control. I thought I had no way out. I was alone, broken, and scared. I fell to my knees and looked up to something I could only trust with my heart. "Ok, God, show me you are real. Show me what you got."

That's when God showed me butterflies!

Jesus said mustard-seed-sized faith can move mountains because our faith is in God, and it's God who moves the mountain! I begged God to reveal Himself to me, and that's exactly what He did.

We all desire to see miracles in our lives. We think of a miracle as something extraordinary and astonishing. But what if our miracle is messy? One thing is sure: a miracle is never messy because God is messy. It is the opposite. A miracle can be messy because life is messy. We are messy. And God is the best source we can turn to in the midst of our mess. We *need* God to come into our mess. And He will, because He is our reason for existing. We have been created to be in a relationship with our perfect Creator. So, my mess led me to God and jolted me straight into His loving arms. If we allow Him to, God will make a masterpiece out of our mess.

Whether we are going through good or difficult times, God wants our faith focused on Him alone. And His miracles will point the way.

While on earth, Jesus performed plenty of miracles. All the miracles He did were to glorify God and prove that He was, indeed, the Son of God. This was also the case in my early walk with God—He used several miracles to get my attention and prove that He was exactly who He says He is. He knew we were about to embark on a long and hard journey together, and He would need me to stay the course. He would need me to have faith, stay focused, and not get distracted.

Since the day I gave my life to Christ, in my weakness, my hope has waved back and forth like the ocean; but my faith, grounded in my Savior, has been solid as a rock. He continues to give me beautiful—and sometimes messy—miracles to sustain my faith and keep me on course. And He has used the most precious gift to light up my path and keep my eyes on Him. I can't always see what is around me or where I'm going. But I can follow the flickers of light and cling to my faith that tells me, "He will meet me every single time. Until I reach home—heaven."

Sometimes God will hide His will from us while offering little sprinkles of hope along the way. In Genesis 12, God tells Abraham to start walking, but, He says, I'll tell you later where to go. God is always testing our faith—our faith to believe the miracles He has for us. Sometimes, He hides His will so we can grow, mature, and be tested in our faith and loyalty. God wants us to leap out in faith and have eyes to see the miracles in our everyday life.

This is my hope for myself. And this is my hope for you.

Have you ever read a book or watched a movie where an angel appeared in a relatable form? This is how God has spoken to me through many great miracles.

Shortly after I gave my life to Christ, something magical happened inside my heart—an explosion of sorts. God radically changed me. That is the best way I can explain it. He changed everything about me. Of course, I still looked the same, but what was inside became a new creation. The most radical and noticeable difference was my new set of eyes. I was finally able to see through an eternal perspective and see the light in this dark world. He just had to show me how.

I often talk about "Chasing Butterflies"—let me explain. God revealed Himself to me through these beautiful creatures, and now they are lighting my path home.

In one difficult season, I was doing all I could to cling to God and trust His promises for my life. It was a beautiful fall day. The weather was incredible, and my baby and I were both taking a nap in my car—it was our safe space. I had the windows down; the only noise was the birds singing and the trees blowing in the wind. When I woke, I was amazed at the most extraordinary blue butterfly sitting on my window. It wasn't startled or scared. It just sat there in complete peace, giving me minutes to observe its splendor. I had never seen a butterfly that close up. That was the moment I started seeing God's promises for me with an eternal set of eyes—depicted in the beauty of butterflies.

God finds the most incredible and precious way to draw us to Him. He knew I would need a constant reminder of my new life and His love for me. He knew I was weak, and this world is tempting and dark. He knew I would need something so sweet and powerful that would ultimately signify His ever-present connection to me. So I began "Chasing Butterflies." It was like I had been moving in slow motion through this life, and suddenly, I was on the move at great speed.

As time went by, butterflies were everywhere in my sight. My love for these beautiful creatures grew stronger by the day. I knew each was a sign from God—a constant reminder to keep me on course. God is so clever. He showed me so many great miracles. There is one I would like to share with you today.

After I gave birth to my daughter, I had an IUD—a form of contraception—placed in me. I had the IUD for about a year, and it was fine. Then one day, I started to have a lot of pain on my left side. I went to the doctor, who ordered an ultrasound to find out why this was happening. The doctor told me my IUD had shifted into my uterus and needed to be removed that day.

I was in a season of struggling with my faith, wanting to believe God so badly but filled with so much doubt. I wanted to believe in all the miracles He was showing me. I wanted to believe He was real. But I had so many voices in my ear telling me the opposite—that my butterflies were imaginary and a coincidence. The hardest part of believing in God was that I felt so undeserving. Why would God think I was so special?

The doctor removed my IUD. She told me I would need time to allow my body to heal before having it placed again. The procedure was quick, and I was able to leave and go about my day. I had plans to go to the mall afterward to pick up a few items. As I was walking through the mall, I was praying and talking to God. To be honest, I was doubting God.

Maybe it's all in my head.
Maybe God is not real.
Maybe I'm crazy.

Then, as I was walking through the mall, I saw butterflies everywhere! I was awestruck at how butterflies were in every blink of my eye. As I was walking, the voices in my head were getting louder and louder, repeating,

You are not special.
You are not important.
You are not enough.
It's springtime, and that's why butterflies are everywhere.

As I was walking, I suddenly felt that I needed to go to the restroom. The doctor had explained that I would have bleeding and cramping for a couple of days. This is where it gets personal. As I walked into the restroom, my eyes filled with tears, my heart in despair, and I just wanted to hit the floor and cry. I felt so defeated and confused. I sat down on the toilet, and I looked down. There it was. In blood. A perfectly painted butterfly with a cross in the middle.

I couldn't believe my eyes. I sat there in complete amazement. I was so happy. Shocked. At that moment, I told God I fully believed Him, and nothing could ever convince me otherwise. God gave me the most precious gift that day. A miracle. I will never doubt Him again. God is real and beautiful, and

He loves me so much. He loves me so much that He gave me an impossible miracle to cling to during those moments of doubt. The rest of the story is that I never bled another drop. Not one drop. The entire world will try to convince me that God is not real, but I know differently. He revealed Himself to me that day in the most miraculous way.

Blood represents life. And there is power in the precious blood of Jesus. The blood of Jesus brought us back to God. Romans 5:9 reads, *Much more surely then, now that we have been justified by his blood, will we be saved through him from the wrath of God* (NRSVA). Every bondage and chain will terminate in the blood. The blood of Jesus can pull down strongholds because we are invoking His very presence in our lives. His power is in the blood.

Before earth and people were ever a thing, God had determined in His heart that He would send His Son to die on the cross for us. Yes, He died so that we could live. How wonderful it is to trace the scarlet thread of the blood of Christ woven throughout the Bible and our lives today! How much more wonderful that I got to experience its power personally. Yes, God thinks I am that special, it's His blood that gives life, and He used blood to reveal Himself and His power to me.

After that day at the mall, butterflies became even more cherished and precious to me. It was like God and I had a secret together. I was chasing God, and He was chasing me.

God wants us to keep our eyes on Him until we reach heaven. He opened my eyes to the beautiful butterfly to light up my path and keep me on course. My flickers of hope, I like to call them. He wants us to stay heavenly-minded. This is the true definition of a Miracle Mindset. It's seeing God in everything and in everyone.

God wants us all to keep our hearts and minds on things above. He wants us to treasure the heart of heaven. Heaven is our forever place to be with Jesus, and I am so excited to chase my beautiful and sometimes messy butterflies until I reach His loving arms. Heaven is home, and heaven is where I long to be.

I have this hope... I truly believe that God loves me. I felt so lost and abandoned for a long time. But God reminded me that He still has plans for my life and will finish what He started. This is proof—what a miracle to be shared. God is so faithful. I can testify to that. I can testify that even in my mess, there is a God who loves me and will never abandon or turn away from me. God loves you that much, too.

God will finish what He starts. He has a plan and a purpose for each of us. He doesn't care how qualified or educated we are. He will give us everything we need to fulfill His mission. I had nothing to bring to the table when God called on me. Absolutely nothing. But He gave me the tools and resources I needed. He gave me a vision that was just between us. God is not looking for perfect people; He is recruiting willing hearts. Just be willing. He will give us just enough to stretch our faith and keep us relying on Him. My faith is concrete even when my hope is lost in the sea. God wants us to trust Him. Let go of the fear by remembering what He's already done. Trust Him!

Now faith is confidence in what we hope for and assurance about what we do not see (Hebrews 11:1 NIV).

God handed down a vision to me—new life. It's beautiful and hard and almost always messy, but I will not give up.

My mindset is to believe and see God in everyone and everything. This is a miracle. We are all God's miracles.

Miracles take time.

Waiting is hard.

Don't lose heart.

Hang on.

God is working.

His time is so much better.

God is with us in the waiting, and He will give us these little miracles to sustain us and keep us on course. Hold tight to the vision. The road to get there is uncertain, difficult, and messy, but keep your eyes on Jesus and the vision He gives you. Just like Abraham, we are to "go." Trusting and believing.

> *And the Lord answered me:*
> *"Write the vision;*
> *make it plain on tablets,*
> *so he may run who reads it.*
> *For still the vision awaits its appointed time;*
> *it hastens to the end—it will not lie.*
> *If it seems slow, wait for it;*
> *it will surely come; it will not delay."*
> (Habakkuk 2:2-3 ESV)

> *The Lord makes firm the steps*
> *of the one who delights in him;*
> *though he may stumble, he will not fall,*
> *for the Lord upholds him with his hand.*
> (Psalm 37:23-24 NIV)

The world may not understand something that is just between you and God. But no matter how messy it looks to the world, how hopeless you feel your condition is, or how much you would like to give up, look for the miracle. Because God is in control of our world. Listen for His voice and do whatever it takes to follow His plan through, even if that means walking alone for a time!

See past the messy. See past the broken. See through the eyes of God. And see a miracle. Give God the control, and He will make a BEAUTIFUL miracle out of you.

FINDING THE MIRACLE IN DESPERATION

by Kelley Rene

Jacob—the son of Isaac, grandson of Abraham, and one of the fathers of the Jewish nation—lived a life of turmoil. His story fascinates me for a variety of reasons. In Genesis 27, we read a scene of deception woven by Jacob's mother, Rebekah. Although Jacob was the second-born, Rebekah worked to ensure that Jacob received the blessing intended for his older brother, Esau. Lie upon lie eventually earned Jacob the blessing from his father, but it would cost him a lifetime of angst, including Esau's threat to murder him.

A few verses later, Rebekah again meddled in Jacob's life, orchestrating a mission to save him by manipulating Issac into sending Jacob to find a wife amongst Rebekah's brother's—his Uncle Laban's—family. On his journey, Jacob experienced a dream in which God declared His blessings over Jacob from atop a ladder reaching to the earth, upon which angels ascended and descended. Genesis 28:20-21 tells of the bargain this dream prompted in Jacob. *"If God will indeed be with me and protect me on this journey, and if he will provide me with food and clothing, and if I return safely to my father's home, then the Lord will certainly be my God"* (NLT).

In the next chapter, ironically, Jacob fell victim to his uncle's deception. The family drama that unfolded rivals modern novels, pitting Jacob against his father-in-law and leading to Jacob running away with his wives and the livestock he'd spent twenty years earning. As Jacob left and began his return home, he recognized that it was time to address his other family feud: the fight with his brother Esau. When he sent a message ahead asking Esau for his favor, Jacob received word back that Esau was on his way with 400 men. Jacob was terrified and devised a plan to protect his wealth and those he loved most. Then he turned to God in prayer. *I am not worthy of all the unfailing love and faithfulness you have shown me, your servant...O Lord, please rescue me from the hand of my brother, Esau. I am afraid that he is coming to attack me, along with my wives and children* (Genesis 32:10-11 NLT). Years of deception, strife, and undeserved blessings had humbled Jacob, and he begged God to save him and his family. Jacob was desperate.

But God.

Jacob was *alone in the camp, and a man came and wrestled with him until the dawn began to break. When the man saw that he would not win the match, he touched Jacob's hip and wrenched it out of its socket. Then the man said, "Let me go, for the dawn is breaking!" But Jacob said, "I will not let you go unless you bless me"* (Genesis 32:24-26 NLT).

Jacob's naturally stubborn and rebellious personality worked in his favor that time. He held on and refused to give up. For all he knew, he'd be dead in the morning once Esau caught up with him.

Desperate times require a heart that recognizes our need for God and a determination to hold onto Him until we receive our miracle. It may not come today. It may not come tomorrow. But we must determine to keep our eyes fixed on Him until He answers.

> *"Your name will no longer be Jacob," the man told him. "From now on you will be called Israel, because you have fought with God and with men and have won"* (Genesis 32:28 NLT).

The following morning Esau warmly welcomed Jacob and his family home. God performed yet another miracle in Jacob's life, and his next actions indicated the heart change that had occurred. Jacob built an altar and named it El Elohe Israel: The Mighty God of Israel. He was finally willing to recognize and accept the God of Israel as his own.

The Latin word for "desperate," *desperare*, means "to lose all hope." God wants to step into your desperate moments and bring you hope where there is none! *Yes, my soul finds rest in God; my hope comes from him. Truly he is my rock and my salvation; he is my fortress, I will not be shaken* (Psalm 62:5-6 NIV).

James 4:8 says, *Draw near to God, and He will draw near to you* (NKJV). If you are desperate for a move of God in your life, lean into Him. Cling to Him. Don't let go until you receive your miracle.

· ·

DeAnn Alaine

DeAnn Alaine is an award-winning co-medienne from Orlando, Florida, whose call is to bring joy to the world! She is happily odd with an absurd perspective on music. Right now, you can head over to Spotify, iTunes, Apple Music, and the like to hear some of her comedic songs: *Mama Trauma, Keep Your Clothes On, Thankfully,* and more! Whether through musical comedy or her carwash comedy show Suds & Superstars (which can be seen on YouTube), DeAnn is sure to bring you a grin and belly laugh! She is the CEO of ComeeDeAnn Productions LLC and the creator/direc-tor of the sitcom, *Fade Away,* with the anticipated release in the spring of 2024 on streaming platforms everywhere! DeAnn is the voice of Sparkles the Starfish and Elsie Algae in Christ Clubhouse on Tubi TV! She is also a regular contributor to Women World Leaders magazine *Voice of Truth* with her article, "Red Carpet Ready." So go ahead to her website and book her for your next comedy event! You can reach DeAnn at www.deannalaine.com or deannalainespeaks@gmail.com

P.S. It's true that she was a nurse turned comedienne. Her career can be summed up in the comedic song, *They're All Dead.*

IDENTITY CRISIS

by DeAnn Alaine

I'm not a writer. I'm not an actor. I don't even pretend to be. I am a comedian. But little did I know the Lord was calling me to a new title.

In 2021, a friend encouraged me to volunteer at the International Christian Music and Film Festival (ICFF) in Orlando, Florida. I didn't know I was signing up to serve with professional camera people, actors, singer/ songwriters, movie makers, producers...you get it. I didn't pretend to belong there; I just knew the Lord wanted me there.

The steps of a man are established by the LORD, and He delights in his way (Psalm 37:23 NASB). I knew I had heard from my Shepherd. *My sheep listen to My voice, and I know them, and they follow Me* (John 10:27 NASB).

During the event, this dynamic woman approached me and prophesied that I would return to this event with a show of my own. "Look around," she continued, "these are your people, and you belong here. Hi, I'm Evangelist Shannon Liddle." Shannon is a TV producer and show host nominated for her work on *Speak Life!*

Moments later, noticing a table with three ladies sitting in front of an audition room, I heard the Lord say, "Offer them snacks." How could I have known this small gesture would result in receiving a VIP invitation to dinner and an opportunity to walk the red carpet? *Lord! Red Carpet? This isn't who I am!*

I heard God quote Himself to me. *"For I know the plans that I have for you,"* declares the Lord, *"plans to prosper you and not to harm you, plans to give you hope and a future"* (Jeremiah 29:11 NIV).

Do you remember the prophecy Evangelist Shannon Liddle spoke over me?

Fast forward to January 2022. The Lord said, "I want you to take an acting class."

It seemed strange, but of course, I said, "Sure!"

I am NOT an actor; I would not assign myself this task. That's how I knew it was Him. So I signed up for a faith-based acting class taught by Ashleigh Ann Wood and Frankie Kovar. One of our assignments was to memorize a monologue and perform it the next week. The following week, I'm standing on stage working a comedy routine I attempted to convert to a monologue. As a comedy set, the audience laughed. As a monologue, it really stunk. My teachers asked me where I got the material.

"I wrote it myself." Then, as if to offer an excuse, I added, "I'm a comedian."

At the end of class, Frankie announced, "IF YOU ARE A WRITER, you need to be writing movies to be produced. This isn't an acting class by itself; it's a production company. We need scripts!"

I totally shrugged him off! *That's not me.*

That Sunday as I lay in bed, I talked to God. "I don't write anything like what they're looking for. I'm not even a writer. But if you want me to write something, I will."

Seconds later, He whispered, "I want you to write a workplace sitcom about a funeral home. Everyone faces death. I want your show to give people permission to laugh through life's darkest moments."

Y'all, I don't know how to write a script! I don't even know the software to write a script. I would need characters and names and stuff. I didn't even know that was called a character breakdown!

I said to Jesus, "Please grant me the knowledge, wisdom, and understanding that I need to move forward in your time and not in mine."

He took me straight to His Word, *For the LORD gives wisdom; from his mouth come knowledge and understanding* (Proverbs 2:6 NIV).

One day later, while Tammy Hanson—an actress and Christian sister—was driving us to acting class, I sensed I should talk to her about the TV sitcom idea. I had just finished writing the breakdown for a character named Tess, and she was the only person I could see performing that role. With Tammy's "Yes," I knew the time had come for the show—*Fade Away*—to be created. The Lord provided me with my Tammy Gift. She would come over just so I could talk to her about dialog and have "pretend conversations" between these crazy characters out loud!

All the while, I kept saying to the Lord, "This isn't who I am!"

I could hear Him giggle at me, "Oh really?" *Therefore if any man be in Christ, he is a new creature: old things are passed away; behold, all things are become new* (2 Corinthians 5:17 KJV).

Singer-songwriter and actress, Jill C. Lewis, stood right in front of me, and the Lord nudged me to speak to her about the principal character, Blanca. I'm pretty sure she wet her pants from laughing so hard. A few days later, the Lord nudged me again to speak with actress Soontaree Jaisin-Simms.

"I was just asking the Lord for an opportunity to perform in a comedy!" Her response made me smile.

How amazing to have the Lord as my casting agent!

When I spoke to Alyssa about the role of Sarah, she mentioned that when she was a young girl, her family turned down an opportunity for her to have an agent in Los Angeles. All these years later, the Lord was offering her a chance to act. The identity the Lord was carving out for me was helping create more avenues for identity change in those around me!

One at a time, each actor was added. Not by my own will, but by His. He placed His hand on each person I asked. *Trust in the Lord with all your heart And do not lean on your own understanding. In all your ways acknowledge Him, and He will make your paths straight* (Proverbs 3:5-6 NASB).

I slowly began to understand that choosing a miracle mindset was helping me change from identity crisis to identity confidence.

A simple brochure was my only visual aid while giving my 3-minute spiel at ICFF 2022. They all groaned with disappointment when they learned the script wasn't yet finished. "I was hooked after 30 seconds," said one of the agents. I promised to reach out to them when the script was completed. That's another miracle altogether.

I had never pitched anything in my life. How did I know what to say? *When they bring you before the synagogues and the officials and the authorities, do not worry about how or what you are to speak in your defense, or what you are to say; for the Holy Spirit will teach you in that very hour what you ought to say* (Luke 12:11-12 NASB).

My thoughts were changing from *This is not who I am* to *Who am I becoming?* Learning how to shift to a miracle mindset takes time!

The painful season of *delay* can also help facilitate a miracle mindset. For two months, *Fade Away* was delayed. I felt like Joseph. One day he's a teenager with a fantastic dream; then you turn the page, and he's rotting away in prison. Yes, I am dramatic. But it was during the delay that the Lord accomplished the greatest work in me. It was in the delay that the Lord provided me with the two best writers for the show—award-winning writer Jaclyn Whitt and comedian and host of *The Clean Comedy Podcast,* James Creviston. My writers and I promise you will be laughing!

By May 2022, it was clear. The prophecy had come true! I returned to ICFF with a show—*Fade Away*—to pitch to industry professionals.

Amber Butaud of 4 The One Studio was one of the producers at ICFF. She's business-minded, stunning, intimidating, and the big surprise, HILARIOUS! The best part? She loves Jesus! We enjoyed some special moments at the festival. As soon as the script was done, I flew to Texas to spend some real time with Amber and her incredible team.

The time had come for Zoom meetings and location scouting. I believed by faith that I was equipped to accomplish tasks I had never done before. *Yes, DeAnn, you are the creator and director for a future hit sitcom called Fade Away, about a third-rate funeral home!*

While writing the script for the pilot episode, I randomly named the flower company Flower Power. I had no idea there was already a flower store called Flower Power in Polk County. The owner permitted me to use their name and even gave me access to their shop and cool Flower Power vans! Their outdoor space served as the perfect location for a restaurant. He and his team were a joy to work with.

One evening, realizing I'd overlooked a minor recurring role in the show, I called up my brother-in-Christ, Christian comedian Cary.

"Hey, Sis, tell me you got something for me!"

My jaw hit the floor. "I do!" I exclaimed. "Let me tell you about a character in *Fade Away*."

He said "YES!" to the role. Y'all, he lives in Texas, and I live in Florida. I called for one reason, but God had another purpose in mind. "What do you need to get the show off the ground?"

God put the word in my mouth. "Money!"

"I can make that work." Cary provided funding for props, lights, food, the camera operator, and the sound crew.

It was late July 2022 when the enemy showed his unwelcome presence, daring to speak to a daughter of the King: Fade Away *is going to be a tremendous flop. It's going to die before it is ever created. You are never going to find a funeral home that will allow you to film at their business.*

The devil is a liar! *When he lies, it is consistent with his character; for he is a liar and the father of lies* (John 8:44b NLT).

The enemy continued his verbal assault. *You can't direct. You don't have the right to direct. Who do you think you are? You don't know anything that you need to know!*

But his attack was a blessing in disguise! It gave me the insight to understand what my identity really was. The liar did the same thing to Jesus when he said, *"If you are the Son of God, throw yourself down. For it is written: 'He will command his angels concerning you, and they will lift you up in their hands, so that you will not strike your foot against a stone'"* (Matthew 4:6 NIV).

Sometimes being a prayer warrior comedian means I get very mouthy! I declared, "I am a director! I am a writer! I am a location manager! I am able to do exceedingly, abundantly above what even I think I can do because of the power of Christ at work within me! Devil, KISS MY GRITS!!!"

Two days later, I pulled a muscle in my lower back while getting out of bed. Suddenly, I needed help doing everything! The enemy never fights fair, and I will never expect him to. When he attacks with that kind of tenacity, I know I am on the right track. But Jesus is so cool! He showed me the identity of the enemy and the location of his weaknesses. During the two weeks of recovery, I was invited to view a funeral home, a potential filming site. Wild horses couldn't keep me away from that appointment. But the drive alone made me *look* like wild horses had dragged me there! My husband is such a careful driver, but it didn't matter. Pain is pain. While hobbling through the funeral home, talking with the management team and owner, the pain in my back felt like I was a ping pong ball being smacked by cactus trees. It was in that moment I got the "YES" from the funeral home.

Today is the first full day of filming. Oh, wait, the enemy strikes again. Big surprise, right? My script supervisor backed out. One of my assistant directors backed out the night before filming, and we were filming in four locations on that one day. Filming at two locations in one day is a lot; four is nearly impossible. What was I thinking? Oh, I know—with God, all things are possible!

Did I sleep well the night before? *No.* I had a prop delivered to my door at 1:00 AM, the morning of filming. I reminded the Lord, the King of kings, that I am not a morning person. Uh oh, is that my next identity change?!?! Let's just stick with one identity crisis—I mean identity defect—at a time!

I have the greatest husband. He anointed me with oil and prayed over me for the task at hand. "Take one step at a time and just breathe," he reminded me.

I don't know how Jesus did it, but He empowered me with the feeling I'd been directing for years. Accomplished actors told me they didn't know I could direct. Truth is, I couldn't!! It was all the Lord! He gets the glory!

"Is this what you want me to do with my life?" I asked the Lord. "To bring you glory through directing?"

This is only one stop on the way to where you're headed.

Hearing His response, I suddenly felt extremely small and humbled. I ducked into a corner at the funeral home and cried. "Who am I that you are mindful of me?" *What is mankind that you are mindful of them, human beings that you care for them?* (Psalm 8:4 NIV).

When asked by cast and crew whether *Fade Away* was a Christian show, I replied, "*Fade Away* is for the world, to bring joy where it's needed." The truth is, it's not, but I am a Christian director. We prayed over the day, prayed over the food, and made sure that if people needed prayer, they knew who to go to. One of my actors commented to my husband that he had never heard a prayer like that over food. He wasn't sure if he was supposed to close his eyes or keep them open. He chose to keep them open, just to see what he hadn't seen before. Another actor, after leaving the set when done for the day, returned to talk to me. Ten minutes later, I'm standing next to my husband when he starts to cry, "I've never felt so appreciated and treasured on set before." He handed me a bundle of cash to ensure *Fade Away* would continue.

On another occasion, two crucial crew members were absent. Immediately, others filled in the gaps, like Tammy, Jill, and Jessica Adams, who plays the hysterical role of Savvi. Y'all are in for such a treat! They stepped into my chaos and brought peace. I have learned this one thing: Desperation is a great place for miracles to happen. Having a miracle mindset puts you in a position to EXPECT His hand of providence to move!

When Amber previewed the pilot, she reacted, "DeAnn, you are what sells the show! How can you not put yourself in it?"

Just when I felt my identity secure, I blathered, "That's not me! I don't do that! I'm not an actor!" Oh, no! I just fell back into the trap of my old mindset.

"You're a comedian! You can act! You get on stage all the time, and that's what you're doing!!!" She was adamant.

I think I'm gonna puke. Is that a little too real?

In one moment, I felt like King David, the conquering hero, and in the next moment, I was hiding in a cave! NOOOOOOOO!!!!!!!!!!

Oh yes, back to work on that identity. Having a miracle mindset and the ability to find peace in the chaos usually involves other people. And Jesus! But for me, it involved the chaos of my thought life and what my heart chose to believe. I was not capable of doing what the Lord called me to do. Knowing that ahead of time prepared my heart and mind for an identity change!

To me, *Fade Away* isn't just a show; it's the fading away of my old nature in exchange for a new one.

> *For I am about to do something new. See, I have already begun! Do you not see it? I will make a pathway through the wilderness. I will create rivers in the dry wasteland* (Isaiah 43:19 NLT).

"And...ACTION!"

THE MIRACLE OF GOD'S GIFTS

by Julie T. Jenkins

We are all created in God's image.

So God created mankind in his own image, in the image of God he created them; male and female he created them (Genesis 1:27 NIV).

Just the thought of all that God is can be so overwhelming! It may cause us to question, How can I possibly be made in His image?

The word "image" means that we resemble God, not that we are His clones. In fact, there are incommunicable and communicable attributes of God. The incommunicable attributes are those which belong to God alone and will never become present in our own lives. For example, God is:

- Omnipotent—He is all-powerful
- Omnipresent—He is everywhere at all times
- Omniscient—He knows everything
- Sovereign—He has the power, authority, and wisdom to do anything
- Transcendent–He exists above all

Praise God for all that He is!

But at the same time that we praise Him, we should recognize that He made us to resemble Him; therefore, we are to acknowledge and hone the gifts He has graciously given us. For although we are not clones of God or each other, we do all carry God's DNA.

When you look in the mirror, what do you see that resembles God? Perhaps you are:

- Creative
- Joyful
- Peace-loving
- Wise
- Discerning
- Gracious
- Faithful
- Generous
- Compassionate

These are not only attributes of God, but they are gifts He shares with us. Our God is so big—His attributes are beyond our human comprehension. And anything good within us is a reflection of Him. All that we are is God's gift to us, and all that we become through His power is our offering to Him.

> *There are different kinds of gifts, but the same Spirit distributes them. There are different kinds of service, but the same Lord. There are different kinds of working, but in all of them and in everyone it is the same God at work* (1 Corinthians 12:4-6 NIV).

Every gift from God is given for a purpose. And that purpose is not for our own gain, but so that we can fulfill our role in the body of Christ.

> *For just as each of us has one body with many members, and these members do not all have the same function, so in Christ we, though many, form one body, and each member belongs to all the others. We have different gifts, according to the grace given to each of us. If your gift is prophesying, then prophesy in accordance with your faith; if it is serving, then serve; if it is teaching, then teach; if it is to encourage, then give encouragement; if it is giving, then give generously; if it is to lead, do it diligently; if it is to show mercy, do it cheerfully* (Romans 12:4-8 NIV).

As members of God's family made in His image, we each have a responsibility to nurture our gifts and use them to their full potential. The miracle of God's gifts to His body is that they all fit together like a puzzle. Together, we all possess the needs of the whole!

I know NOTHING about farming. For me and my family to eat, we need farmers to use the skills God gifted them with. When I get sick, I rely on the gifting of doctors, nurses, and medical technicians. And although I work in ministry, spending my days empowering and teaching others, I also need and depend on others using their gifts to hold me up.

Praise God that He never lets anything fall through the cracks! He has provided all we need within the body of Christ through the miracle of the gifts He gives us.

. . . .

Lisa Hathaway

Lisa Hathaway is a lover of Jesus that has a passion for the least of these. Her heartbeat is to see those who need a second chance experience the tangible love of Jesus. She has learned to worship through suffering as a special needs mom, recent breast cancer survivor, and survivor of a tragic car accident within a two-year time span. Suffering has been intertwined in her story, and she wants others to experience the sweetness of God through some of the most difficult things in life. She comes alive when others experience the redemptive love of Jesus.

Lisa resides in Lexington, NC with her amazing husband of 21 years, Everett, and her precious children, Savannah, Andrew, and Luke. She loves family and pouring love into others.

She has an MBA, and through the adversities in life, she stepped into God's calling on her life and is currently attending Liberty University to pursue her degree in Clinical and Mental Health Counseling. She currently works at The Oaks Therapeutic Community, a Christ-centered counseling and wellness consulting community that is dedicated to supporting individuals on their journey toward worth and wellness while finding the value God gives each person.

Sweet Miracle

by Lisa Hathaway

Today, we hear the word "special" so often. It is a word that has a different meaning for different situations. In my life, the "miracle of special" came through my son, Luke Avery Hathaway.

It was 3 a.m. one night in late spring when I abruptly arose from bed after hearing an audible voice.

"This baby is no mistake, and he is no accident." The voice was soft, gentle, deep in tone, and spoke so clearly. I knew it was God speaking directly to me.

But how could I make any sense of what He was saying? I was on birth control and had just had a baby five months earlier. My cycle was not even late. I was so confused, but I could not shake the feeling. I went to work that day, and during my lunch break, I bought a pregnancy test. Within seconds, the double pink strips appeared.

Pregnant.

Oh my gosh! How can I have another baby right now? I sobbed. My emotions got the best of me as I tried to process it all in my head and heart. God knew exactly what He was doing. I could not see it at the time, but the months and years to follow would reveal this precious child to be one of

God's sweetest miracles in my life.

I went through a period of adjustment, coming to terms with the fact that God wanted me to have another child. I was a CEO of a local non-profit and was under a significant amount of stress. Day in and day out, I balanced and navigated the intricate details of the multimillion-dollar business. And here I was, big and pregnant.

In October of 2008, I found out that the baby growing inside me was a boy. I was excited but still trying to figure out how I could possibly manage another baby with my demanding job. I would learn that I needed to relinquish control to God. A simple thing to do, right? Sometimes our flesh takes over when we feel out of control, but God always has better plans than we do. He sees the end from the beginning. Although I fully trust that God's plans are better than mine, I couldn't begin to understand at that moment what an amazing future He had for our family. God was in the midst of creating Luke in an extraordinary way that would showcase just how perfect His plans always are.

Luke Avery was born in February of the following year. It was a quick but difficult delivery. My epidural didn't even have time to take effect. He was the smallest of my three kids, weighing just eight pounds and five ounces. He was just precious, but I still wondered how we would manage. My husband and I brought our newborn son home to meet his 14-month-old brother, Andrew, and his 2½-year-old sister, Savannah. Busy was an understatement for our lives. I took Luke to work with me after just two weeks of being home—after all, I was the CEO and needed to be present. I already felt bad for taking the time off I had. It was an unhealthy balance, but that was my frame of mind at the time.

We took Luke to the pediatrician for his four-month check-up. As a mom of three, I had noticed some things were a little off; for example, he didn't turn toward sounds on his left. I also felt in my spirit that something was different. Those still small voices—discernment through His Holy Spirit—should not be ignored.

God whispered Zephaniah 3:17 into my spirit: *For the LORD your God is living among you. He is a mighty savior. He will take delight in you with gladness. With his love, he will calm all your fears. He will rejoice over you with joyful songs* (NLT).

Luke's body was often rigid, and his hands clenched, so the pediatrician suggested physical therapy to help. We followed her instructions, then turned to an early intervention organization. A neurologist prescribed an MRI. Walking through all of this was so hard. Although the process was fast, there were times when it seemed excruciatingly slow. *How could this be happening to us? What did we do to have a special needs child?* So many uncertainties swirled around in my head.

When he was six months old, the doctors diagnosed Luke with Spastic Quadriplegia Cerebral Palsy. We were advised to build a wheelchair ramp because our son would never walk or talk. He was missing white matter on the right side of his brain. I was devastated driving home from the hospital that day. I was angry. I was in disbelief. I was physically sick. I had not envisioned my life like this. Questions popped into my head by the hundreds. This sweet child, this gift that God gave us, was going to face a difficult road, and I couldn't fix it.

I needed to regroup. Somehow, I needed to be a strong mom who would both advocate for and care for my son. My husband was so understanding. We talked, cried, and yelled, but most of all clung together. You see, parents of special needs children have a higher rate of divorce. The strain on a family and marriage such a journey causes is astronomical. It was a miracle God gave us the will to fight for us and the blessing of staying together.

After realizing that Luke was aspirating on his saliva, doctors placed him on honey-thickened liquids. For four years. Every drink had to be thickened. Any food that had a thinner consistency also had to be thickened. The time, the money, and the preparation for this were often overbearing. Due to the many appointments and challenges, I left my corporate job and became Luke's full-time caregiver. God sees all and knows all. He had this path planned all along. He sees the end from the beginning even when we cannot. I stand in amazement at how God works. His promises are true. Steadfast. Unwavering.

As that first year progressed, the neurologist ran more tests and requested genetic testing for Luke. *How could there be anything else wrong? Haven't we experienced enough?*

Four months after the geneticist drew the blood work, the test came back: Luke had a very rare genetic disorder. It was an extremely rare 6q27 chromosomal deletion. I asked the doctor for the name of the disorder.

He laughed, "We will just call it *Luke's Disorder.*"

I knew God ordained that moment. The uniqueness of Luke was coming full circle. God knew EXACTLY what He was doing when He created Luke. When God spoke to me in the wee hours of the morning about this child being no mistake, He was preparing my heart.

We've walked through years of therapy: occupational, speech, and physical therapy. We've incurred major medical expenses. But God always provided. Luke was later diagnosed with autism and he also experiences migraines and seizures. He was delayed in every milestone. But God has always been in control: by wearing braces on his legs, Luke was able to take his first steps. And I learned that my plans and expectations have nothing on what God can do.

Over time as I reflected on Luke's plight, God started downloading fresh revelation to me. When I feared the realities of being a mom to this precious boy, God gently reminded me, "Lisa, my daughter, you are not alone. I created him exactly the way I want him."

The life verse I gave Luke when I found out I was pregnant with him is Psalm 139:13-15, *You made all the delicate, inner parts of my body and knit me together in my mother's womb. Thank you for making me so wonderfully complex! Your workmanship is marvelous-how well I know it. You watched me as I was being formed in utter seclusion, as I was woven together in the dark of the womb* (NLT).

I continue to stand amazed at how God reached down even before Luke's special needs were identified and spoke truth to my heart.

God stayed so near to me as we walked through the first year of Luke's difficult life. He reminded me how we are all created for a purpose and are the handiwork of God—beautiful pieces of art molded into being by a master potter. One day I pondered how "special" and unique each of us is and what makes Luke Avery different from everyone else.

Maybe he can't hold my hand like my other kids, but he holds my heart with his eyes.

Maybe he can't wrap his arms around me to give me a hug, but he wraps me in his love when he lays his head on me.

Maybe he won't be as independent as my other children, but I will be his independence.

Maybe he won't be able to sit up, but that means I will always be able to hold my baby.

Maybe he won't be able to express himself with gestures and emotions, but I will have his coos, smiles, and cries to tell me what he needs.

All children have "special" needs. They just come in different packages.

When a present is unwrapped, you have no idea what you are getting. Each gift holds something different. Different surprises. Different experiences. They will not be the same. I will enjoy this "special" child God gave me and see him through the eyes of Jesus. Each child is a miracle, a gift, a special treasure. I strive to learn from Luke and my other two kids every day. Each one of them communicates in their own unique way. Each one will worship Jesus in their own "special" way.

Each of my three kids is different. That is what makes them "special."

As I've walked through this process, I've stood alongside grief in complete amazement—the grief of my expectations of having a "normal" child. God gives happiness and can also give heartbreak. In the heartbreak, we need to grab His hand ever so tightly. When we do, we will experience growth. When trials come into our lives, God provides a way for us to hold steadfast to the miracle on the other side. God is a compensating God; He will always give us exactly what we need. As I continue to walk this journey, I am committed to giving God all the glory He is due. For Luke's life is nothing short of amazing.

Right after the neurologist told us Luke would not be able to walk or talk, I believed there was something more. God spoke so clearly to my heart:

I created Luke exactly how I wanted him
I gave him the eyes that look deep into your soul
I gave him the joy that you could carry in your life every day
His smile will melt the hardest of hearts

Because I am your God, I knew Luke would be here to give Me glory
You will watch him grow into whom I want him to be
Even if he can't touch you or reach for you, his soul will serenade over your life
I will give you the peace and courage to walk with him
I have called you as his mom to stand in the gap for him
No matter what you face, I will give you grace each day
He will touch lives and exude my joy
I will show you how to celebrate life no matter what you thought it looked like.

Luke is taller than me now, and sometimes it just takes my breath away. This child whom God spoke to me about is now 14 years old. He walks, talks, laughs, and is fearless in so many ways. He speaks life over others. He is aware of others around him and loves them unconditionally. Luke brings such joy to others with his intentionality as he constantly asks others about their day and sees other people despite their situation. I vividly remember how he ran to a homeless friend, offering the biggest hug. A hug that crossed socioeconomic status and exemplified what the love of Jesus looks like. That homeless man, who became our friend, talked about Luke's hug until the day he died.

As I look back on Luke's 14 years of life, I stand in complete amazement at what God has done and continues to do in his life. Luke lives with daily challenges, but he is nothing short of amazing.

This sweet miracle is my son. In all that he has done and accomplished, I still to this day notice the smallest of miracles in his life. I do not know what the future holds, but I am clinging to the promises of God. Hebrews 10:23 says, *Let us hold tightly without wavering to the hope we affirm, for God can be trusted to keep his promise* (NLT).

Take God at His word. Seek His face in all you do. No matter what the diagnosis, the storm you face, the trials you walk through, or the fire you feel engulfs you, God is there. He will shield you, protect you, and hold you so close. When God gives you a miracle, He will remind you of all that He can do. I know that if He parted the Red Sea, He can do so much more for us. That is how much He loves us.

Keep your eyes focused on seeking His face. The gratefulness that comes from the suffering in our lives is a miracle. To have gratefulness is to experience God in all parts of our life. Knowing there are no mistakes or mishaps when God is in complete control is comforting. No matter the debris thrown at you as if by a tornado, God will keep you under the shadow of His wings. Psalm 91:4 says, *He will cover you with his feathers. He will shelter you with his wings. His faithful promises are your armor and protection* (NLT).

The miracles God has for you might be small, big, or even difficult to recognize, but oh, how sweet they will be. Have gratitude for the miracles. Every day is a miracle with Jesus.

THE MIRACLE OF JOY

by Julie T. Jenkins

> *Rejoice in the Lord always. I will say it again: Rejoice!* (Philippians 4:4 NIV).

Joy is indeed a miracle! Let's face it: the world constantly throws us curve-balls that threaten to distance us from joy, and yet, by resting in God and trusting in His control and wisdom, we can walk through any chaos while we rejoice in the Lord.

Have you ever stopped to think about the majesty of God? He is SO BIG! David, the shepherd-boy-turned-king, did. He pondered God's greatness unceasingly—writing songs and prayers to and about Him. When David underwent trials, after he fell into temptation, when the walls were closing in on him, and when the heavens were shining their glory on him, he praised God for His goodness and might!

David longed to build God a temple, but God told him, *"You are not to build a house for my Name, because you are a warrior and have shed blood"* (1 Chronicles 28:3 NIV). Yet, although David was prevented from living out his heart's desire, he went forth in joy, expecting and trusting God for the miraculous. When it finally came time for the temple to be built, David passed the baton to his son Solomon. As offerings poured in that allowed him to envision the finished project, David joyfully praised God:

"Praise be to you, Lord,
  the God of our father Israel,
  from everlasting to everlasting.
Yours, Lord, is the greatness and the power
  and the glory and the majesty and the splendor,
  for everything in heaven and earth is yours.
Yours, Lord, is the kingdom;
  you are exalted as head over all.
Wealth and honor come from you;
  you are the ruler of all things.
In your hands are strength and power
  to exalt and give strength to all.
Now, our God, we give you thanks,
  and praise your glorious name."
(1 Chronicles 29:10-13 NIV)

God has given His children the miracle of operating in joy no matter what our day brings—because our joy is rooted in Him alone. When we ponder the greatness of God, we can rest in the fact that God is sovereign—He is in control of all that is and was and ever will be. God is our provider—so we can trust that the One who holds all things in His hands and loves us above all else will always ensure we have everything we need. God is wise—so despite whatever issue we face, we can go forth in joy, knowing He will lead us down the right path.

Let me encourage you today to live like David! Spend time each day pondering the goodness of God by reading His Word daily, seeking to uncover His miracles in Scripture. Then, ask Him to show you His workings as you go through your day, praising and trusting Him even in the unexpected.

Finally, begin to praise God with every breath. When we take our eyes off the world and keep them fixed on our amazing Father, we will experience the miracle of His deep-seated joy as it infiltrates the corners of our life.

Don't wait another moment. Take time now to ponder God's goodness. The joy of the Lord IS your strength—and it is miraculous! Grab onto it today, and never let it go!

. . . .

CAROL TURKO

Carol Turko has spent most of her life on the Canadian prairies, where she raised her two sons. She then followed her dream to move west to the beautiful Okanagan Valley in BC, Canada.

Carol has a passion for downhill skiing, but it is not to be compared to her fiery passion for sharing the Word of God and leading others to Christ. Carol co-pastored with her former husband in Manitoba and was part of leadership at Street Love Ministries, serving as Director of Families.

Because of her pastor's heart that longs to see people healed, set free, and equipped, Carol has taken several physical and emotional divine healing courses. And because of God's grace, she has seen many people healed, including herself. Carol has served on multiple prayer teams and led many Bible study groups. She loves praying for people, seeing them set free, and pointing them to Jesus, the way-maker and miracle worker.

Carol welcomes anyone to reach out to her with their prayer needs or for encouragement. Email her at setfree4hisglory@gmail.com

Bulldog Faith

by Carol Turko

It had been years since I'd ridden a bike. Still, I was looking forward to joining an adventurous group on a trail ride along the Okanagan Lake. I'd heard a lot about the BC Rail Trails and always wanted to take a bike ride on one of them.

The thought briefly crossed my mind that maybe a 30 km ride from Penticton to Okanagan Falls might be too much for my first time on a bike in years. But the group promised to go slow and stop for breaks along the way.

The ride was exhilarating, and the view was breathtaking. The Okanagan Valley never disappoints. We strayed from the highway and followed the lake on a narrow, partly shaded dirt bike trail that snaked mostly along the flat shoreline. At noon, when the sun turned the warm air into a scorching hot day, the pavement veered right. Uphill. The heat motivated us to keep pedaling, and we stopped less frequently than planned. In fact, we only stopped one time, for just a few minutes.

When we reached our destination, we ate lunch and then headed back the way we'd come. Pain throbbed in my neck and back from clenching the bike handlebars tightly and hunching over for so long. But I kept pace with the other bikers. I didn't want to get left behind.

Once home, I expected the pain to dissipate. However, the next morning when I woke up, the pain was still there. It was constant. And it wasn't just sore muscles but nerve pain. Planning to make an appointment with my family doctor, I scrolled through Facebook. A video advertisement for Life Works Family Chiropractic in Kelowna talked about not only alignments but also nerve pain relief. *Lord, are you trying to tell me to go to this clinic for treatment?* I made an appointment.

During my visit, an x-ray revealed I had degenerated cervical discs with a lot of damage to my vertebrae and calcium buildup. A nerve test confirmed my pain registered a nine on a scale of 10, and it was constant. It was determined that I should begin treatments immediately. The chiropractor, Dr. James Whillans, explained the extent of the damage to my neck. He indicated it wasn't necessarily related to age. He even told me the damage could have occurred during my childhood.

My life has been riddled with incidents that could have caused or contributed to the damage. My parents told me that, as a baby, I'd hold the crib rail and jump up and down. Higher and higher, I jumped until I flew up and sailed out of the crib onto the floor! Then there was the time I tumbled head-first down the wooden stairs to the cement floor in the basement of our house.

Growing up, I was a bit of a tomboy. I tumbled off bikes, fell while playing sports, and had a few major wipeouts downhill skiing. I even rolled my vehicle in a horrible accident once. It was a miracle my friends and I survived my car flipping front to back several times. And, of course, I can't forget the toboggan incident; as an adult, my children talked me into trying their flying saucer, and when they shoved me off, I flew over an embankment onto a frozen creek. The force was so hard my winter hat actually popped off my head like a cork on a wine bottle. My head slammed down onto the ice, and my neck connected with the ridge of the flying saucer. Ouch! Yes, it hurt. I actually saw stars. There was also a period when I lost everything and spent some time sleeping in my car, which undoubtedly kinked my neck. Yes, I have definitely had many possible contributing factors to the diagnosis of degenerative cervical vertebrae. But God always brought me out of each mess. Now, I prayed under my breath, Lord, do it again. Rescue me from this pain.

The visits to the chiropractor did lessen my pain, but unfortunately, I did not have insurance to cover the recommended three appointments per week. *Lord, I can't handle this pain or financial strain. I need a miracle, Father.*

Shortly after, I saw a video online by Pastor Amy Keesee Freudiger about healing. After watching the last of the videos, I ordered her book, *Healed Overnight.* Holy Spirit was moving me toward receiving healing and restoration of my cervical spine.

I realized I had to change certain mindsets to receive my miracle, which included believing God loves me and that I am worthy of healing. I also had to eliminate the guilt and condemnation I carried, acknowledging that as a child of God, healing was mine—not because of anything I've done but because of what Jesus did for me on Calvary. So I began to search for teachings on knowing who I was in Christ and receiving in my spirit a sense of my right standing with God.

I believed a lie about myself. I was a divorced woman, and because of that, I felt below God's standards and unworthy of receiving anything from Him. I did have great faith for others when I prayed for them, but believing in and for my own healing from this neck pain was going to be a challenge. The Bible says in Proverbs 23:7, *For as he thinketh in his heart so is he.* (KJV) I thought, in my heart, that I was worth less than most people. I felt ashamed. I felt, in my heart, that I had to really work hard to be approved by God; that He blessed others, but my blessings might be withheld because of my past. I had this tape recorder going on in my head that said things like, "You're stupid, unloved, not worth listening to, shameful, dirty, and always going to fail."

Throughout my childhood, teenage years, and my first very short marriage, I had been a victim of abuse. I remember exactly when a spirit of shame came into my life, and I did not know what to do about it. I kept the secret inside and told no one; it festered and took over my life. My parents recognized how withdrawn I was, and it frustrated them, as I never told them why. I did not want to tell them my friend's father had molested me. I felt ashamed. I began to lose myself and who God intended me to be. I saw myself as trash and started to act like it. I stopped excelling academically in school and poured myself into sports. I was hurting inside, but on the outside, I portrayed myself as a very strong girl. The wounding began to take over my heart and dictate who I was. This wide-open emotional wound, I found out later through counseling, stunted me emotionally and spiritually, not allowing me to progress past the age of 12. This vulnerability attracted negative people, abusers, and narcissists, and I was defenseless and unarmed spiritually to stand against this type of spirit. God eventually led me to healing and restoration from those abuses.

My second husband and I lost everything, then we divorced. I found myself homeless and sleeping in my car. In came the shame again, along with depression, feelings of being a failure, and fear of poverty. Having faced this before, I now recognized this as a spiritual battle, and I was armed with the knowledge of how to fight. However, it took a while to overcome, and within a couple of years, I found myself now with this damaged cervical vertebrae to add to the fear, depression, and shame. With all these negative emotions, I found it hard to press in and believe for the healing of my neck. The pain and emotions were speaking louder than my faith.

To counteract the lies of the enemy and my soul, I poured myself into the Word of God and meditated on scriptures about God's love. I worked to break the mirror of lies the devil was continually trying to get me to look into and, instead, focus on the mirror of God's Word, embracing the beautiful daughter God says I am. Finally, the negative voices were silenced enough so I could start searching for God's promises of healing.

I have learned that sometimes we fight battles, gaining understanding and victory so we can minister to others. If we let Him, God will turn our pain around for good. He calls us to a unique purpose and destiny, and that is often the very area Satan attacks us in—the territory we are to claim. I have been called to a healing ministry, both emotionally and physically. I rejoice each time I see someone healed. It is always fresh and exciting when God uses me to see the finished work of Jesus in someone's life. Now it was my turn to get physically healed.

Proverbs 4:20-22 says, *My son, pay attention to what I say; turn your ear to my words. Do not let them out of your sight, keep them within your heart; for they are life to those who find them and health to one's whole body* (NIV). God gave me a revelation: taking this verse as directed would work just like a doctor's prescription. God's Word is medicine. We can believe its power will cure and heal us. His Word is no respecter of one person over another; it will work the same way for one as it was for the other. Just like medicine is no respecter of one person over the other and is usually taken 2 to 3 times a day, so we should take God's Word, confess it (say it out loud) over ourselves repeatedly each day, and believe in its power. So I took this to heart.

I followed the instructions laid out in Pastor Freudiger's book. I began my day by honoring the Lord with the Lord's prayer. Holy Spirit led me to personalize it by expounding on each line.

I would pray something like this, but each day would be a little different:

Our Father, who art in heaven. "Lord God, you are our Father. You are my Father. I have a family of believers who I can fellowship with. Thank you for being my Father; thank you for sending your Spirit to dwell inside of me. You know me, and I am never alone because you are always with me."

Hallowed be thy name. "Lord, you are holy. I reverence your name. Forgive me if I have taken your name in vain, Lord. Because of your goodness and majesty, the heavenly angels sing holy, holy, holy is the Lord God almighty; who is and was and is to come. Lord, I love you, and I sing of your holiness with the angels."

Thy kingdom come, thy will be done, on earth as it is in heaven. "Lord, you said because I accepted you, the kingdom of God is within me; therefore, the anointing for healing is within me. By faith, I release healing to my vertebrae; bring healing right now, Lord; I release this healing to every area of my body. In Jesus' name."

I continued in this way until I completed praying through this scripture found in Matthew 6:9-13 and Luke 11:1–4.

After a few days, I felt the presence of the Lord in my room as soon as I started to pray. His love, His goodness, and His glory would overwhelm me. When I felt His presence, I thanked Him for sending His Word and for healing and delivering me of my own destructive ways, which of course, were all the incidents that may have led to the damage of my vertebrae. *He sent His word and healed them and delivered them from their destructions* (Psalm 107:20 NKJV).

I thanked Jesus for Isaiah 53:5, *But He was wounded for our transgressions, He was bruised for iniquities, the chastisement for our peace was upon Him, and by His stripes we are healed* (NKJV).

During the day, I praised God, saying: *Praise the Lord, my soul, all my in-*

most being, praise his holy name. *Praise the Lord, my soul, and forget not all His benefits—who forgives all my sins and heals all my diseases, who redeems your life from the pit and crowns you with love and compassion, who satisfies your desires with good things so that your youth is renewed like the eagle's* (Psalm 103:1-5 NIV).

I meditated on Romans 8:11, *But if the Spirit of Him who raised up Jesus from the dead dwells in you, He who raised Christ from the dead will also give life to your mortal bodies through His Spirit who dwells in you (NKJV) and* Matthew 8:16, *They brought to Him many who were demon-possessed. And He cast out the spirits with a word, and healed all who were sick* (NKJV), declaring, "Because I am born again, the same Spirit that raised Jesus from the dead lives in me, and He gives life to and restores perfection to my mortal body. Thank you, Lord, for your Spirit in me, for fixing what is broken and in need of repair".

I believed that because *Jesus went about all Galilee, teaching in their synagogues, preaching the gospel of the kingdom, and healing all kinds of sickness and all kinds of disease among the people* (Matthew 4:23 NKJV), I, too, was included in Jesus' healing.

For almost a month, I woke up in the mornings and spent quiet time personalizing the Lord's Prayer and claiming the Bible verses as my own. Throughout the day, I spoke to my cervical vertebrae, saying, "Listen here, cervical vertebrae, line up with the Word of God and be healed. Be separated with no calcium buildup. Vertebrae, be healed in Jesus' name."

A year had passed since I started treatments with Dr. James. I no longer had constant pain and was down to one weekly treatment. It was time for another evaluation. This time, the doctor stared at the X-ray, puzzled.

"Is there something wrong?" I asked.

He answered, "Carol, there seems to be a line between some of your cervical vertebrae. It appears they are separating."

Surprised yet ecstatic, I replied, "Well, thank you, Dr. James. And thank you, Jesus."

He looked at me and said, "No, Carol, it's the other way around." Later he told me, "You do know this was medically impossible. Your neck vertebrae were badly damaged—bone on bone. Not only are they separating, but they are regenerating."

Praise God! Thank you, Lord.

It wasn't until I decided to take a stand and use what I call "Bulldog Faith" that my miracle began. I had to be consistent. I had to stop letting the sickness occupy my territory and my thoughts. I made a conscious effort not to give voice to the pain or the condition. It was not easy at the beginning, but it was worth it.

The Bible says my body is the temple of the Holy Spirit. Sickness and disease had violated my temple, and the enemy of my soul was trying to rob me of a good life. I had to fight. I had to bombard myself with God's truth. Being consistent was the key. I was determined to receive my healing. I developed Bulldog Faith and would not let go of the vision of seeing myself healed and free of pain.

The victory of my healing gave me confidence in the Word of God. Now, I am more sure of who God is and that He loves me. He is my healer. I also have a new boldness and confidence when I pray for others.

God recently used my testimony to reach a young mother. My miracle of healing, which I had written about on Facebook, popped up when she searched "healing from pain." Her 11-year-old daughter needed God's healing touch, so she reached out to me, and I agreed to pray and believe with her for her daughter's healing. I felt led to ask if she or her daughter had ever received Jesus as their Lord and healer. She said she believed in God, but they had never heard to actually ask Jesus to forgive them and invite Him into their lives. After I explained salvation to them, they both renounced all works of darkness and thanked Jesus for forgiving them. They invited Jesus to come into their hearts (lives) to be their Savior and Lord and fill them with His Spirit. This young mother said she would share this powerful experience and pray with the rest of her family. Then, filled with tears, I prayed for healing for her daughter. Afterward, they both committed to believe for healing. I began mentoring them, and they started attending a church only a few minutes from where they live.

Still, after all the MRIs, CAT scans, and painful tests, the doctors didn't know what was wrong. I suggested that perhaps it had something to do with her daughter's spinal column. So they went to a chiropractor, who discovered a reversed curve in her spine—a completely reversible condition. The chiropractor announced, "I'm going to get in there and do the adjusting, and God will take care of the rest. Everything will start to heal."

She is still in the middle of her treatments, which will take up to six months, but the doctor urged, "Once I'm done, I want you to spread her story."

I praise God for my miracle and for that young girl's upcoming miracle.

It's so important to listen to that wee small voice inside—the voice of God—and follow His direction. We know from the Word of God that the Lord is no respecter of one person over another. What He's done for me, He'll do for you.

I pray for you as you read this chapter—that you, too, will receive your miracle. Reach out in Bulldog Faith, stand on the Word, and don't be moved by what you see. Stay faithful, listen to God's voice, and receive your miracle.

FINDING THE MIRACLE IN SICKNESS

by Julie T. Jenkins

It can be difficult to recognize the miracle in sickness. But if we have a Miracle Mindset, God will allow us to see beyond the scope of our circumstances and give us a glimpse into heaven. Two miracles God will make apparent to us as we deal with an illness, whether our own or a loved one's, is our ever-deepening dependence on Him and His all-enduring orchestration of love at work through those around us.

Having our physical body fail can move us into a state of despair as we feel increasingly helpless, losing control of even the most basic aspects of life. Sometimes, God will meet us in our sickness with His healing touch. But other times, when our bodies continue to fail, we can still trust that He is working in our lives, and with a Miracle Mindset, we can recognize that when we are weak, God is strong. The Apostle Paul spoke of this understanding in 2 Corinthians 12. Scripture tells us he had prayed for healing three times, having suffered greatly from some sort of ailment. But instead of being healed, Paul received a word from the Lord: But he said to me, *"My grace is sufficient for you, for my power is made perfect in weakness."* (2 Corinthians 12:9 NIV).

When we are at our end, we have no choice but to rely on our God. And when we do, He will always come through. God repeatedly promises that He will be with us through hard times.

"Be strong and courageous. Do not be afraid or terrified... for the Lord your God goes with you; he will never leave you nor forsake you" (Deuteronomy 31:6 NIV).

God has said, "Never will I leave you; never will I forsake you." So we say with confidence, "The Lord is my helper; I will not be afraid" (Hebrews 13:5-6 NIV).

When we have a Miracle Mindset, we can indeed proclaim that the Lord is our helper. But not only is the Lord our helper, He also sends an army of warriors to help care for us.

God strategically placed unique giftings within each of us so we can care for each other.

There are different kinds of gifts, but the same Spirit distributes them. There are different kinds of service, but the same Lord. There are different kinds of working, but in all of them and in everyone it is the same God at work. Now to each one the manifestation of the Spirit is given for the common good (1 Corinthians 12:4-7 NIV).

As believers, we belong to the body of Christ. And as part of this whole, we were each sent here on a mission: to care for one another. Perhaps at no time is the complexity and precision of the body more apparent than when one of us falls ill. That is when our God, who is in complete control, orchestrates a team of medical professionals and loved ones to care for the individual fighting an illness. Just think about the team that rallies around someone with an illness: there are the scientists who have worked for years developing life-saving and comfort-giving medications, the nurses who have trained to be at an ill person's bedside, doctors who have spent countless days and nights studying and preparing for their profession, not to mention the pharmacists, technicians, first responders, support personnel, caregivers, and even untrained loved ones who set everything aside to do what is most important at that moment. Talk about a dream team!

When our bodies fail, and they all will, we need not fear. In fact, we should respond in expectation—because miracles will soon be exposed. With our minds set on Christ, He will give us the miracle of peace as we lean on His strength and wisdom. And, as we place our worn-out bodies in the hands of those He has positioned around us, we will witness the true miracle of God's giftings at work in and for His children. All orchestrated by our miracle-working God!

. . . .

KAT PENNINGTON

Retired to the Florida panhandle, Kat and her husband enjoy spending time with their children and grandchildren. Their mini-schnauzer Trooper keeps them busy when the kids aren't visiting!

Kat was a Certified Professional Photographer with the Professional Photographers of America (PPA). A recipient of four national *Kodak Gallery Award of Excellence* and an international *Kodak Gallery Elite Award,* she was an invitational guest speaker at two International PPA Conventions as well as several regional conferences.

In addition to her photography career, Kat participated in community service. A volunteer firefighter for 15 years as well as a member of the Red Cross Disaster unit, she also founded her hometown's first annual Independence Day Fireworks celebration.

During her husband's military assignment to Paris, France, Kat graduated summa cum laude from a French university. While they were stationed at Northwestern State University, she earned her MA and taught graduate-level photography courses as an adjunct professor.

Kat became a Stephen Minister in 1994 and was trained to provide one-to-one care for those experiencing a difficult time in life. Currently, she and her husband lead their church's Marriage Mentoring Ministry, sharing their passion for living marriage God's way.

FIGHTING FOR NOTHING

by Kat Pennington

Our God is a healer. The body usually comes to mind when someone uses the word "healing," like when Jesus made the blind see and the lame walk. But my story isn't about physical healing—it's about emotional healing. Regardless of life's circumstances, I have learned that faith can conquer fear, and peace is possible if we surrender our lives to God.

GROWING UP FEARFUL

I grew up in a dysfunctional home. My mom was a paranoid schizophrenic, and my dad used his military service as an excuse to leave our family. My parents were estranged for many years and then divorced when I was a teen.

My mom took my younger sister, Lisa, and me to church when we were very young, and she read Bible stories to us throughout our childhood. When I was about eight years old, my Sunday school teacher told us that Jesus was God. I can picture my eyes rolling as I thought, *Of course He is!* I was already well aware that Jesus died on the cross for me to take my sins away so I could live with Him forever. When I was old enough to read the

Bible for myself, I began to feel God speaking to me through His Word and assumed since He loved me so much, He would grant me the blissful life I imagined. I can't recall a time when I didn't know Jesus as my Lord, but I can think of a time when I chose not to trust Him.

Since my dad had abandoned us and no one knew where to locate him, I had an unfilled longing for a father figure. When I was young, I overheard a heated argument between my parents. "I'm sorry I ever had a family," my dad yelled, "I never wanted any of you." His words haunted me for decades.

My mom's contempt for my dad bled into me, and I disavowed my dad and appointed God as not only my God but also my earthly dad. Of course, kids naturally want to please their fathers, so I tried hard to do the same with God. I even built a little rock altar for Him in my backyard!

Because of Mom's mental illness, she, Lisa, and I moved often. Through my teenage years, feelings of helplessness churned into fear, magnified by the circumstances in our house. Since my mother was reclusive, Lisa and I didn't know where or who to turn to. We watched mental illness devour our mother. I silently questioned if it was genetic—something I was destined to inherit.

As things at home worsened, I reached out to Mom's family for help. Unfortunately, they chose to ignore the signs of her declining mental health. At the time, mental illness was even more taboo than it is today. It was embarrassing. In refusing to admit my mom's condition, her family turned their backs on her, my sister, and me. Lisa and I had nowhere else to turn.

During our high school years, my sister and I lived a secret life. We hid things more and more from the world. We lived a lie of *Just fine* when people asked how we were. We assumed if someone took our mom away, we would end up in a state ward, separated from each other forever. Fearful of that possibility, we vowed to stay together no matter what it took.

I had acquaintances but no real friends. I couldn't ask anyone to come home with me anyway because of Mom's condition. The thought of her illness being hereditary began to hang around in my mind as I wondered, *If my friends knew me and knew how my life is, would they leave me, too? Why me? Why does everyone else seem to have it all together?*

Whenever Mom had a rough day, seeing things that weren't there and hearing "people walking in the attic," we knew it would be a long night. The three of us moved into a little rental on a quiet street where neighbors nodded to say "Hello" but never initiated a conversation. Years later, I discovered it was rumored around town that my mom was a reclusive alcoholic. But she wasn't; she didn't drink at all.

Most kids come home from school to a safe place. My sister and I wanted that too, but life inside our house posed daily challenges. The battle against an invisible world within my mom's mind made her paranoid and security-conscious. As a result, she kept the house dark and quiet. Lisa and I never knew what we were going to face. At times, we would come home from school to find our mom sitting on the floor in a corner, wildly chewing gum. Her eyes would be large and glassy as she spoke in frantic whispers. Sometimes her hair was in pigtails, and other times it was simply uncombed.

Mom kept the windows in our home covered with aluminum foil and newspapers. And we had to keep the lights off so the "people in our attic couldn't film us." Taking quick showers in the dark and whispering through cupped hands became the norm for us. We had a TV but kept it off to be spared from "seeing our life portrayed in commercials" created by "the people in the attic who were filming us." Mom randomly switched out the dinner plates in case we were trying to poison her. My Mama. Her illness crushed my heart while emotional scars of hopelessness and fear settled into my mind. I wondered how long it would be before I got sick.

My dad served in the military during my parent's marriage of over 17 years. He knew about my mom's illness at the time of the divorce, and also knew about her right to a percentage of his military retirement. Too ill to realize what she was doing, my mom was deceived into declining her portion of Dad's retirement pension, *agreeing* to accept one child support payment instead of two. Of course, Dad hired the lawyer. My dad showed up at the lawyer's office to sign the divorce papers but never took the time to even say "Hello" to Lisa and me. Then he disappeared again.

Since my mom was too ill to work, she, Lisa, and I lived on the money my dad was ordered to pay to help support one child. Needless to say, times were tough. So I took a minimum-wage job at a grocery store to pay for our food. Still, I didn't always have enough money to pay for what it took for us to survive, so I just took what we needed. Our mom was oblivious to where the groceries would suddenly appear from. Stealing groceries led me to years of requesting God's forgiveness over and over. Although I repented and fully understood God would forgive me, I kept asking Him because I couldn't forgive myself.

Even in her confusion, my mom was protective and repeatedly proclaimed she would not allow anyone to harm us. I didn't see the people she saw and couldn't hear the voices she heard, but they were real to her. I was at a loss for how to bring peace to our lives. Many nights Mom would shuffle up and down the hallway in her bedroom slippers, carrying a kitchen knife in her hand. With my bedroom door closed, I would lay in bed with Lisa beside me, both of us too scared to make any noise. Being the oldest, I slept closest to the door—just in case.

I made a plan that if our mom came into my room with the knife. I would try to stop her while Lisa ripped the foil from the bedroom window, broke the glass, and ran—not looking back, no matter what. Then I'd follow—if I could. Some nights I'd pray we would live through the night. And honestly, there were some nights I would pray we wouldn't. *Was this God's plan for me? For us?*

My life seemed to spin out of control as my mother's illness progressed. Time passed, the turmoil in my home worsened, and my pleas for God to rescue us went unanswered. Because of such a volatile home life—watching everything I did and every word I said—I learned to hide my emotions well. As a result, I had difficulty expressing feelings and became convinced I was unworthy of being loved by anyone. My sense of stability was gone, and rejection, fear, and despair became my typical emotions.

I blamed my dad for leaving us in the chaos, concluding that everything would be different had he stayed with us. It seemed like not only had my earthly dad deserted me, but my Heavenly Father was doing the same. I began questioning God, *When are You going to help us? There were many more questions. Have I not loved You well enough? God, why did you even create me?*

When Lisa and I graduated from high school and moved out of the house, the money from the child support stopped. Having nowhere else to go, my mom moved in with her mom, my grandmother. It was then that my mom's family finally acknowledged her illness. I thought it would be a relief to know she was getting help, but instead, life for my mom got worse.

Those were the days of electric shock treatments, where a patient's arms and legs were forcibly strapped to a table as an electric current flooded their body. My Mama. Again, my heart broke. Every time she returned from a psychiatric ward, she was a mere shell of a person, talking in a slow mono-tone and walking with her arms straight along her side. She would improve for a while, and then her illness would rear its ugly head again.

Seeing my beautiful mother go in and out of psychiatric wards devastated me. *Where in the world was Jesus during those times?* I attended church and constantly talked with God through all those years of turmoil, but He didn't supply the answers I expected. *How could I surrender to His control when I was afraid of the further hurt He might allow to come to Mom? And me?* I had lost trust in everyone, and, sad to say, God was on top of that list.

I continued to wear a smile in public and search for a purposeful life. Driven to prove my self-worth, I became an overachiever. However, despite receiving awards and accolades from my fellow professionals, family, and friends, old insecurities and feelings of inadequacy destroyed any value I had for myself. Although my prayers, patience, and hope stretched over many years of believing God would rescue me and restore my mom's mind, He didn't do either.

CONSEQUENCES

I became weary from mentally fighting against my mom's paranoia and schizophrenia and the never-ending fear of following in her mental-illness footsteps, a path that I believed would surely lead to the loss of my sanity. I even wondered why God would give me two precious sons. I loved them intensely but didn't think I was worthy of being called their mom. My insecurities had no boundaries, even as I raised my children.

My fear of becoming mentally ill led to a *preventive* prescription drug abuse regime. Trusting in myself for a cure rather than continuing to wait on God, I resolved I could *preempt* mental illness by taking *preventive* drugs. By following my plan, I was able to lead an outwardly successful life, raising my children, volunteering for community service, and owning a successful business. I was good at acting, and no one in my community or family could see how much I struggled emotionally.

Then one day, I just couldn't do it anymore. The years of unanswered prayers to rescue me had ripped a jagged cut in my emotional being, and the fear of my children waking up one morning *to find my body alive, but my mind gone* overtook me. Concluding I would never be *normal,* and before my children were forced to live with what I had grown up with, I intervened in God's timing and tried to take my life. It was a selfish, desperate attempt to find peace. I could see no other solution as years of mental anguish had worn me down. I don't remember doing this, but my doctor told me I had written the word *normal* on myself. That's all I wanted, to be normal like everyone else.

After healing in the intensive care unit, I was taken to a drug facility to recover from years of prescription drug abuse. The sound of the doors locking behind me as I walked into the facility was a painful flash of insight into what I'd done. My efforts to prevent mental illness resulted in the very thing I fought so hard against—being locked away in a facility. Though it was a drug recovery facility and not a psychiatric ward, it felt the same to me. Panic set in, and I cried out, begging desperately to go home. But things in life are not always that easy, and because of my choices, I could not just walk away.

HEALING

God knew exactly where I was, and He never left my side. During an intense counseling session on the third day of my in-house treatment, a doctor grabbed me by the arms and shook me hard to get my attention. Then he looked directly into my eyes and said, "There *is* no true normal. You are fighting for *nothing!*" Those simple words hit me with such force and clarity that I could feel God speaking directly to me through that poor, exasperated doctor. At the moment the doctor released my arms, a feeling of calm washed through my mind and body. The Holy Spirit filled me with His peace—it was unreal and marvelously astounding. Instantly, I knew I had been captured by fear and fiercely battling against a mental illness that had never been my destiny.

After years of suffering from emotional pain, fear, and hopelessness, God miraculously healed me in a single moment. This wasn't just an inward change; it was a transformation that manifested itself on the outside of me as well. I know this because my doctors signed my release from a mandatory 28-day drug recovery program after only seven days. Two nurses celebrated God's miracle with me. We cried happy tears and hugged as I left the facility.

SWEET SURRENDER

For the first time in years, I knew God had been with me every day of my life and longed for me to persevere as I waited for Him to change my circumstances. From that time forward, I surrendered my trust fully to Jesus. I no longer blamed anyone else. It wasn't my mom's illness, my dad's absence, or my fearful mind that robbed me of control. Instead, it was my lack of trusting God to answer me—in His timing. My journey through the chaos would have looked and felt different had I fully surrendered to God in the first place.

BLESSINGS

About my mom: She died—still beautiful and still mentally ill. During her healthy periods of awareness, she was the sweetest woman ever, and I will always be thankful she introduced me to my Lord Jesus. And although her illness continues to baffle my comprehension, I know that her life somehow glorified God. I fully trust His plan, which included Mama's illness.

About my dad: He became a Christian and served on mission trips to Costa Rica. He didn't take care of my sister and me as most dads do, but he did care for orphans who desperately needed a home. He remarried, and when he became feeble, his wife put him in a nursing home. It was there I visited him almost daily—not because I felt I had to, but because I wanted to. It was there where, before he died, all was reconciled and forgiven between us; years of anger melted away. God gave me a bonus miracle.

About my sister: She's a wonderful woman who has a close relationship with the Lord. We're in constant contact and rarely end our texts without a red heart. She doesn't recall much from our childhood, and I count that as a blessing from God.

About the facility doctor: I still remember the name and face of the man God used to speak truth and healing to me. I will always be grateful for his genuine compassion.

About me: I was a prodigal daughter. God didn't give me wealth to squander, but I did inherit free will, which I squandered by deciding to do things my way and in my time. Well, that didn't work out at all. I can't imagine how often God protected me, despite myself. Now, I'm no longer fearful hurt is lurking around every corner as I continue to keep my commitment to trust God and in His timing. I now have the freedom to live with joy.

About God: God is very good! And everything He does, including when He chooses to answer prayers, is nothing less than perfection. He can and will heal our hurts and pains, even the invisible ones we successfully hide from others. God makes Himself easily accessible, *offering* us His peace. He truly is *Yahweh-Raphah*, my healer. He is the healer of everything. He assures me, *"I AM the Lord, who heals you"* (Exodus 15:26 NIV).

THE MIRACLE

We all suffer consequences from the actions of others or ourselves. But through it all, we can believe and stand on the fact that life unfolds in God's timing and perfection. At each and every step, we have the glorious opportunity to choose to trust God, even when circumstances seem impossible. That is being Miracle Minded.

Finding the Miracle in Uncertainty

by Kelley Rene

Uncertainty is that deep-seated feeling of not knowing. Whether we're unsure of an outcome, how we should react in a situation, or feeling doubt or hesitancy regarding a circumstance, being uncertain is something we all encounter.

The Bible is filled with people who faced uncertain times. Joseph was sold by his brothers to slave traders and hauled off to a foreign country. Jonah spent three days in the belly of a huge fish. Paul was shipwrecked on an island and also spent years in prison. As each of these men looked to God for help, God showed up in miraculous ways. In God's timing, Joseph became the right-hand man to Pharaoh; Jonah took God's message to the people of Nineveh, who repented and believed in God; and Paul wrote many letters to the New Testament churches, which later became the very Bible we study today.

The authors in *Miracle Mindset* recount times of uncertainty: injuries and illness, heartache and loss—many stemming from circumstances beyond their control. And yet one by one, as they turned their eyes and heart toward Jesus, their faith grew, their outlook changed, and they experienced joy. They could see God's miraculous hand working in their lives.

Uncertainty is a foggy night when the fuel gauge shows empty, and there's not a car in sight or a gas station for miles. It's a stack of bills piling up on the counter while you hold a pink slip in your hand. And it is an unknown virus spreading like wildfire across the globe.

We've all experienced uncertainty.

Even believers in Christ Jesus face uncertainty. But the difference is we don't face it alone. As a matter of fact, we can trust our sovereign Lord to walk us through uncertain times and bring us through victoriously. *For the Lord is God, and he created the heavens and earth and put everything in place. He made the world to be lived in, not to be a place of empty chaos. "I am the Lord," he says, "and there is no other"* (Isaiah 45:18 NLT).

And because God is sovereign, we can respond to uncertainty with faith. Hebrews 11:1 proclaims, *Faith shows the reality of what we hope for; it is the evidence of things we cannot see* (NLT). We can turn to Him in prayer for protection when alone on a foggy night. We can turn to Him for provision with that pink slip in hand and bills stacked high. We can turn to Him for healing and peace when illness strikes.

He is never surprised by, unaware of, or caught off guard by our circumstances. He wants to step into our calamities and make us whole. *And we know that in all things God works for the good of those who love him, who have been called according to his purpose* (Romans 8:28 NIV). Despite our own uncertainties, as Christians, we know God hears our prayers and answers them. He fights for us.

As 2 Corinthians 5:7 reminds us, we can walk with certainty in this world when we trust God in faith rather than trusting what we see. The miracle that uncertainty leads to is a triumphant faith that stands firm in Jesus Christ in the midst of any storm. Unwavering. Unmoved. Unafraid. Put your trust in God to bring you through uncertain times.

No matter what uncertainties you face, as a Christian, you can stand strong, trusting our sovereign God. Turn to Him. Let Him ignite your faith and give you peace.

SAMIE V. MAXINEAU

Samie V. Maxineau is a proud follower of Jesus Christ who loves her dearly. She is Canadian by birth, Haïtian Dominican by blood, and American by choice. She is the mother of three precious kids worth living for (Xander, Bella & D'Angelo).

Samie had been married to her high school sweetheart, Fred Maxineau, for 17 years.

Holding a Bachelor's Degree in Health and Wellness and having obtained a Master's degree in Health and Wellness Coaching, Samie has now also been a nationally certified Massage Therapist for over ten years. She is currently a Future Senior Cadillac Driving Sales Director in Mary Kay Cosmetics and a best-selling author, contributing to the book *Victories: Claiming Freedom in Christ*.

Samie is passionate about serving others through the purpose God has placed in her heart. She has a heart for marriage and stay-at-home moms, especially those running businesses. Her motto is: fall nine times, get back up one more time. The cross has the final word. Christ is still in the refurbishing business. HE truly can take any broken masterpiece and refurbish it. Have any doubts? Get to know Samie's journey.

.

GREATNESS IS IN YOU!

by Samie V. Maxineau

THE VOICE

Sometimes I hear an internal voice shouting loud and clear that I am not good enough. It echoes like a tambourine welcoming a king to her bride, becoming louder with every step. So I often hesitate to try something new, whether a sport or a new adventure, believing the lie and being concerned that I could never achieve perfection.

But doesn't God say that when we are weak, HE is strong? Doesn't He command us to be strong and courageous and acknowledge Him?

Yes, He does!

As I've battled this voice, God has never stopped finding ways to remind me that I am who HE says I am and that I can do all things through Him, despite any lies I have received from the enemy.

Let me share the story of a miracle that God did in my life when I moved out of the way and trusted Him to work.

ANNOUNCEMENT

I am a driving sales director with Mary Kay, and a few months ago, my company announced a 60-day Face Race Challenge—a competition centered on who could encourage more people to give their honest opinions on the Mary Kay skin/bodycare product. Of course, I said yes, because challenges always help me grow. However, I didn't know how much this particular challenge would make me confront some of my deepest fears.

I love going to the sauna at the gym after a workout. It always relaxes me and is a great way to detoxify the body, and as this was the 3rd week of the challenge, even hanging out in the sauna would offer me an opportunity to speak about my products. When I went to the sauna on this occasion, I met three wonderful ladies. One had a bit of a deeper connection with me. Whatever I shared with the other two ladies resonated with her. She kept nodding and smiling, showing off her pearly white smile. I asked her to be a face model for me. She agreed, then asked me unexpectedly, "Do you know how to swim?"

I promptly and kindly replied, "No, not really. Well, my husband says that when I am in troubled water, I should try to relax and float, just like a frog."

We both laughed, and I continued to explain to her that my husband is an amazing swimmer. He had swum across a lake in Montpellier, Paris. And although he was very scared in the middle of crossing the lake, when he was tired, he turned on his back to catch his breath. In that way, he made it through to the other side while his friends cheered and encouraged him.

Although I was laughing, my fear of swimming was real. That is not unusual among my black friends. Besides fear, many of us don't want to swim because we don't want to mess around with our hair—lol! But facing our fear, and braiding our hair, can help us learn a skill that could save lives.

Research shows that African Americans between the ages of five and fourteen years old are 3.2 times more likely to drown than white children of the same age, even though, before the civil war, more black people knew how to swim than whites.

My new friend and I continued talking, and as if on a mission, she shared about a swimming instructor who was offering free lessons. I listened politely and even agreed to meet the instructor.

Then we both enjoyed the sauna and went home.

SELF-REASONING

Life got busy, but I surely overthought the idea of taking swimming lessons. Still, I did not call the coach, reasoning with myself, *Why is he giving lessons for free? What if I drown? Hmmm... I don't think this is a good idea...he must not be a great instructor. Swimming is super expensive! The last time we put the kids in swimming lessons, it was great, but that 30 minutes was fast, and we needed to buy more packages, and eventually, we had to pause the classes altogether.*

I had all these thoughts constantly running through my head. I traveled to my annual leadership conference and then to another one. Upon returning home, I went to the gym, and the first person I saw was that same friend! Can you guess what she asked me? "How are swimming lessons going? How do you like them?"

I was like, "Ummm.... Hey mama! How are you? Oh my goodness! I actually did not call him!"

She was surprised, asking, "Why? He is a really great instructor!"

To which I replied, "Are you sure? His lessons are FREE!"

She said, "YES! And you actually learn. He is so patient too! In fact, he is here now. Would you like to go meet him?"

With a smile on my face, I replied, "Sure!" Then, I proceeded to the pool area. When I got there, I noticed a few people in the pool with the instructor, Teddy. Their ages ranged from the late twenties up to the sixties. Most of them were fixing their gear—fins, swimming hair caps, goggles. *OK, that's a bit impressive,* I thought. *What's the catch?*

I greeted the new people coming to meet Teddy for the first time; then I introduced myself to him. I told him who had invited me and he asked me for my phone number. Later, he sent the text below:

"All classes are FREE and 1 hour long. Come when convenient. Results are best at twice a week or more. All I ask is: (1) Encourage someone else to take lessons and learn how to swim. (2) If you're on social media, follow Teddy Fayne on Facebook and BlackPeopleCanSwim06 on Facebook, Tik-Tok, and Instagram to keep the movement going. (3) …If comfortable, tell your story, post videos, and tag us… Your testimony will help free others from their fear. 2 Timothy 1:7 - *For God has not given us a spirit of fear, but of power and of love and of a sound mind* (NKJV)."

The verse in the text blew me away. It's one of my favorite verses. It erases my fear when fear comes to knock me down. It reminds me of whose I am when lies fill my head. This verse reminds me that I am a child of God, a daughter and princess of the most High God! He did NOT give me a spirit of fear. I am royalty! This verse reminds me to hold on and push through the fear, obstacles, uncertainty, mud, clouds, and pain. This verse reminds me that I am a warrior! Wow! With just one glimpse of that text, I felt encouraged, reminded, and ready to scuba dive. Lol! Well let's calm down. I wasn't ready to scuba dive yet, but you catch my point. Despite still feeling the fear, I felt like this was my time to stop running. That day was amazing, even though I hadn't yet gotten in the pool. Some of my most troubling questions were immediately answered when I saw how he spoke to people and noticed the graduates in the middle lane, swimming like little black editions of Micheal Phelps' children. They were so confident!

Throughout that day, I imagined my first swimming lesson. I went to the store to purchase goggles and a swimming hair cap. My heart was full. I was excited. A part of me could not believe this was happening.

NEW BEGINNING

I chose to attend lessons on Wednesdays and Thursdays. On my first day, I arrived at the gym prepared to swim. Then I went to class, greeted everyone, and got in the water. The pool is heated, so I did not feel too cold. Teddy has a big bag with fins and other accessories swimmers can use. I found that super kind. He asked me about my size, then found me a pair of fins in his bag. I hadn't found a swim cap yet, so I tied my hair back and proceeded to follow his instructions.

Teddy asked me if I had any past water-related trauma that we should address before proceeding. I replied no. Within 30 minutes of instruction about how to breathe, float, and stop fighting the water, I was floating and swimming a bit. Everything was happening so fast my brain could not comprehend the speed of it all. I have always freaked out in the middle of the pool because I hate water over my head and am so afraid of drowning. How was it that I was passing the middle of the pool without sinking? I knew it was because Teddy was there every step of the way, reminding me that God did NOT give me a spirit of fear. It was so uncomfortable each time I had to breathe under the water, but I kept meditating on that verse.

My shoulders were so tense. Teddy told me to relax countless times. I had to take breaks in between laps because I was getting overwhelmed. But other new students kept telling me I was doing great. Some of the previous students that were there swimming in the middle lane were also encouraging me. It was great, overwhelming, fascinating, and surreal.

Me—Samie Maxineau—swimming!

Right before I began the lesson, I thought it would probably take a year to learn how to take a lap without freaking out in the middle of the pool. Whenever I think about the fact that my legs cannot touch the bottom, I start panicking immediately. Yet, during the lesson, I found myself persisting despite the fear and anxiety within me. God did not give me a spirit of fear, I repeated in my mind. I can do this. *"I can do all do all things through Christ who strengthens me"* (Philippians 4:13 NKJV).

When it got closer to the one-hour mark, and I realized I had survived and surely did not die or sink in the middle of the pool, I started shivering!

I was standing at the side of the pool when I sensed a big wave of gratitude envelope me. I was shaking! Teddy immediately noticed and rushed to ask me if I was OK.

"I am SO GRATEFUL!" I blurted out to him. "I am so grateful. I cannot believe this is happening! Never in a million years did I think I would be here. Maybe when my kids graduate, but not now. Wow! I am so grateful."

Teddy said, "I understand. It's amazing. You got it! You are doing absolutely amazing and have done more than what many people do in their first lessons. Keep coming, keep practicing, and you'll be surprised at what you can accomplish in the pool. Black people can swim. However, a lot of black people believe the lie that they cannot, and so they either never try and discourage others from trying."

On that first day, I attended class for three hours. I received one-on-one attention for about 30 minutes, and for the remainder of the time, I practiced, receiving occasional advice or correction from Teddy. He took two videos of me swimming before I left and encouraged me to share them with my family and friends or on social media if I felt comfortable. I WAS SO EXCITED!!

I just knew my husband and kiddos would probably not believe me when I told them I did a lap without seriously panicking or sinking. And I was absolutely right.

As soon as I got home, I kissed my husband and shouted, "Babe, YOU WOULD NEVER BELIEVE WHAT HAPPENED TODAY!"

He was looking at me, waiting to hear the big news. But instead, I said, "Let me show you something." I turned my phone on and played both videos.

He was like, "OK... OK?"

I said, "Let me play it for you again."

I played it again. And he said, "OK... that's.... nice."

My husband had no idea it was me in the video.

Then I said, "Babe, take a close look. Can you tell who that is? That's me!!"

To which he replied, "Naw..."

"Yes! It's me! Forget the goggles. Take a close look. Remember the bathing suit I bought when we traveled to Hilton Head?"

Then he took a closer look and replied, "THAT'S YOU?"

"Yes! Babe, that's ME!"

My husband said, "WOW! Not bad for black girl! That's really you! What happened to fighting with the water? This is really good, Babe! Good job!!!!"

Then I shared with him all about my experience and how I was so thankful that Teddy and the Word of God helped me face my fear. My husband immediately started asking if Teddy could also train my son and my daughter. He was an instant believer! He knew that if someone could train me to swim in just 30 minutes, he could teach anyone! Fred, my husband, is a great swimmer; he knew how frustrating it was for me not to know how to swim and how frustrating it was for him to try to teach me.

That day was so liberating for all of us.

JOY AND LESSONS LEARNED

During the next class, I had to stop and ask Teddy, "Why? I know this is amazing, but why are you doing this? I am just inquisitive. You are changing people's lives! You are changing the trajectory of their lives."

He replied, "I know."

I said, "Did someone try to kill you in the past; did you almost drown? What happened?"

"Nothing major like that happened! I just got tired of not knowing how to swim! I got tired of hearing the stigma that 'Black people don't know how to swim.'"

Teddy then told me a bit of his history that most people didn't know. A few years earlier, he had given his wife a destination birthday party. About 80 people were present. He said that although it was fun, it was sad to see the people in the water, hardly moving, because they did not know how to swim. Upon his return, he decided to take swim lessons at one of the top swimming schools in Atlanta. He was doing well and started encouraging and giving pointers to his peers. His instructor caught his gift for teaching and noticed his patience. He immediately encouraged him to consider becoming an instructor.

I was blown away by his story. I commend Teddy's instructor for calling his gift out. He surely called the king out of him. I was so inspired! Since then, I have been sharing about Teddy's gift of teaching with everyone. In fact, one of our good friends, currently serving in the army, is now taking a swimming class with Teddy. He has made great progress. One of my client's mother is also in that class. IT'S AMAZING! It's empowering. And it's freeing to learn to do something you never imagined was possible.

In fact, this experience pushed me to explore further what I, a stay-at-home/work-from-home mama, can accomplish in my business. I did not want this euphoria to stop! As a result, my team and I went on to reach goals by the 15th of the month that we normally take until the end of the month to meet. This catapulted us to earn a huge reward—a Chevy Equinox! I did not set my sights on such a big accomplishment, but I simply said, "God, if you allowed me to learn to swim in such a grandiose, inspirational, and

AMAZING way... what else can happen? What else can you do through me? I want to share this with a million-plus people. Growing in discipline will help me do that." And that's what happened! God boosted my confidence, giving me encouragement and strength to speak into the lives of others!

Physically, I was ready to graduate from the swim class within a month, but my mind was still not there. I was still just a bit scared. Then life happened, and I couldn't make it to the graduation that month. However, I did officially graduate the next month, and it was perfect! My family was there. Some of my friends were even there to support me. And I could not have been more PROUD! Proud of my obedience to jump into the Face Challenge, which led me to meet a new client, who opened the door for me to become Teddy's student, and then watching God use me to encourage a community of people by calling out their gifts and motivating them to push through, practice, and get up one more time instead of quitting when failures and obstacles arise. OOH, I LOVE IT!

Anyone can swim. Black people can swim. God did NOT give us a spirit of fear but a sound mind!

It's time to destroy fear. It's time to show the kingdom of darkness and lies that the truth SHALL prevail. God's Word is true. And it is time that we all listen. GREATNESS is in you, whether you see the evidence of it right now or not quite yet! Keep digging, and trust God for the miracle! He has a diamond just for you!

THE MIRACLE OF GOD'S WORD

by Kelley Rene

Growing up, *Guideposts* was a staple in my home. We didn't have much, but one thing my mother splurged on was her annual subscription. The small yet effective monthly magazine presented a daily Bible reading plan with a short description and explanation of the designated scriptures, definitions, and memory verses—one entry each day to guide its readers through the entire Bible in one year.

We'd often come home from school to find our mother at the dining table hunched over her Bible, an issue of *Guideposts,* and a notebook, scribbling notes as she studied. Everyone knew not to disturb her during her afternoon quiet time. But she didn't keep the study to herself.

She had one rule—actually, she had a lot of rules—but one was unbreakable: We were not allowed to do anything, and I mean *anything,* until *our* Bible reading was complete for the day. Our initials in the margin confirmed our compliance. Oh, how frustrated I'd get with her. When I asked to hang out with friends, go to the mall, or even walk to 7-Eleven for a Slurpee, her answer was always, "Have you read your Bible today?"

My mother's steadfast determination to immerse her children in God's Word still astonishes me! She kept her laser-sharp focus on the future blessings she knew we'd reap. No matter how much my brothers, sisters, and I whined, complained, fussed, and fought to avoid reading our Bibles for just 15 minutes each day, she never wavered. Occasionally, I was even tempted to lie my way out of the task, but God knew the truth, so I'd slump up the stairs to my room to read.

I learned of God's provision through the stories of Abraham and Isaac. I recognized familiar hymns and worship songs in Psalms and Proverbs. I identified Lucifer's sin as my own when he allowed pride to consume him. Most importantly, I discovered the precious love of our Father through the birth, life, and death of our Savior, Jesus Christ. Reading through the books of the Bible day in and day out, year after year, laid a foundation of faith in my life that would carry me through many trials.

As an adult, my mother gifted each of us an annual subscription to *Guideposts* to share with our own families. This became a reminder for me to keep God's Word at the center of my family. *[God's] word is a lamp to my feet and a light to my path* (Psalm 119:105 ESV). Reading the Word shaped how I felt about myself in my formative years. It filled me with the knowledge of who God is and how much He loves me as I matured. And over time, it instilled in me wisdom, confidence, and conviction.

I'm convinced I would not be who I am today or as grounded in the truth and grace of God had it not been for that Bible reading plan—and a mother who was relentless in her determination to instill God's Word into the next generation. My mother passed away in 2019; her well-worn black leather Bible with comments scribbled in the margins is such a sweet reminder of her love for us and God's Holy Word.

I now joyfully pass along what I learned from her: Having a Miracle Mindset requires us to be invested in God's Word through daily Bible reading and study. When we are, our hearts will be open to seeing His miracles all around us.

. . . .

ELLIE MCGRAW

Ellie McGraw is a dynamic, fiery, passionate, prophetic voice who loves the presence of God!

From the early age of 9 years old, Ellie audibly heard God's voice. Since then, she has had many interactions with the Holy Spirit as He speaks to her through various avenues. Because of the freedom she has received, Ellie loves to see the body of Christ set free, healed, and delivered.

Ellie has a passion for equipping leaders and raising up champions by offering sound biblical keys to the Kingdom of God. She has spoken and taught in churches in many nations and served on numerous teams. Since 2000, she has had a counselling, healing, and deliverance ministry called FREEDOM TO SOAR (freedomtosoar@me.com). She also leads various mentorship and prayer groups focusing on healing, the prophetic, and prayer.

Ellie writes articles for NewsLetters, has written in Women World Leaders' *Voice of Truth* magazine, and is a #1 Best-Selling Author in the book *Surrendered: Yielded with Purpose.* She leads intercession on a 24-hour prayer line called The Canadian Firewall.

Ellie is a mother to 4 children, grandmother to 14 grandchildren, and resides in beautiful Okanagan Valley in Kelowna, BC, with her husband.

BUSTING THROUGH THE ROOF

by Ellie McGraw

The pain ripped through my lower abdomen, sending what felt like spears throughout my whole front and lower back. I buckled over. It had started a week earlier as a low piercing pain on my right side. My breasts felt engorged, and I wondered if I was finally pregnant.

I was admitted to a small city hospital, and after many tests, the medical staff felt I wasn't pregnant as nothing showed up indicating that I was. I kept telling them, "No, I am quite sure I'm pregnant. Why else would my breasts be somewhat engorged?"

Tests in those days weren't quite like today. In fact, this was before ultrasounds, CT Scans, and pregnancy urine strips. They kept saying, "No, no, you are fine. You are probably having your monthly cycle."

On my third day in the hospital, my breasts seemed smaller again, and I began to think the doctors and nurses were correct in their diagnosis. Everything seemed to have returned to normal except for the slight pain on my right side and low back area. But alas, the medical staff must know best, I reasoned as they discharged me. I was 23 and had experienced a miscarriage two years earlier. I knew I wanted a baby.

When I returned home, my pain intensified. This searing pain now felt very different than anything I had experienced before, and I fell to the floor in the middle of the kitchen, bleeding extensively. Something was definitely happening. Pressure, searing pain, fear, dread, and violent contortions overtook me. Yes, this was all very different!

I called my work to tell them I would not be coming in today. My tall, down-home, country kind-of girlfriend, Brenda, picked up the call. She spoke very firmly, "Ellie, I think you need to call a doctor!"

I told her what had already happened.

With exasperation, she said, "That's it, I'm coming over!"

By the time she arrived, my skin was pale, and I was extremely weak. The blood pooled around my lower half. Brenda grabbed my arm, and we hobbled to the car. We sped away quickly to the hospital.

Once there, things happened at a rapid pace. They took my blood pressure and temperature and ordered tests. All of a sudden, there was no time to waste! I was quickly informed, "You are going into surgery right now!"

When I regained consciousness, the nurse quietly confirmed that I had been pregnant. It was a tubal pregnancy. The tube had burst, so they removed the baby. I was now septic, with infection running throughout my insides. My right tube was removed, and the internal bleeding was swabbed and stitched up.

I lay there crying.

Just two months earlier, I had been raped by two drunken men. I knew both of them but had never been treated like this by them ever before. But ever since then, I had not been myself. The baby was obviously the child of one of my abusers. Which one, I was not sure. This realization brought even more torment and confusion.

I sobbed harder as I tried to console myself through the emotional trauma I now faced. I had never told anybody about the rape, and I didn't expect to receive any support from anyone. Who do you tell about something so horrible? I suffered alone and in silence. Only God knew my tears.

Rather than dealing with my anger, torment, fear, distrust of men, depression, trauma, and confusion, I turned my back on God and ran away into a world of rebellion. Within a few short months, I divorced my husband.

Immediately following, I found myself living with another man for a few years and eventually getting married to him. I was 29, and in the following seven years, I continued to suffer through more pain and trauma as I tried to get pregnant and, this time, keep the pregnancy. I used fertility drugs, only to lose two more babies. Another surgery ensued when it appeared my remaining left ovary might burst. With scar tissue forming inside the only tube I had left, doctors told me to let go of the idea of getting pregnant—it would never happen. I was ready to give up hope. For years I had been trying to get pregnant, only going through one disappointment after another.

Perhaps, I reasoned, my rebellion against God led Him to no longer care about me. Endometriosis began to form, and my rebellion escalated, as did the dysfunction in my marriage (which, years later, eventually morphed into emotional and physical abuse).

I had recently bowed my knee in surrender to the Lord Jesus Christ and asked Him to come into my life. I gave Him all my sin, confusion, shame, guilt, betrayals, distrust, pain, rebellion, pride, disappointments, hurts, anger, rage, depression, and suicidal thoughts. I brought this huge dirty sack to Him, and Jesus gently took it from me. I had finally surrendered to the King of the Universe. I came to Jesus! He would not only be my Savior but also my Lord Jesus Christ, King of my heart!

My husband and I found ourselves going to a home Bible study group with people we had recently met at church. Previously, we had both done many different drugs and lived in rebellion for years, so we were very apprehensive about this new step. As we walked down the sidewalk toward the back door of the house, we pondered many questions. *What will this night be like? What do they do at one of these meetings? Do they just study the Bible, like the title says? Will they accept us? How will we ever belong to this older generation group? How could they possibly understand how we behave and what we have already lived through?*

We were quite rough around the edges. I certainly didn't dress like people I knew that went to church. But we were resolute in our decision to attend. We were going to give this a try.

At the end of the evening, the leader asked, "Does anyone have a prayer request?"

I looked around the room. No one had a prayer request. *Wow! These people must all be pretty perfect if they don't even have a prayer request.*

With my stomach in knots and my heart beating out of my chest, I timidly said, "We would like to have a baby. Could you pray for us?" Then I told them a very small part of my history, leaving out most of the details.

With compassion and great excitement, all of them chorused, "Oh yes, we will pray for you!" And they began to pray for us right there on the spot!

It reminded me of a Scripture in the Bible, *And when they could not find by what way they might bring him in, because of the multitude, they went upon the housetop, and let him down through the tiling with his couch into the midst before Jesus. And when he saw their faith, he said unto him, Man, thy sins are forgiven thee* (Luke 5:19-20 KJV).

Just like those friends Luke wrote about, our new friends proceeded to bring us to Jesus, ripping the roof off the place, so to speak, in order to do so. They prayed, busting through the roof.

> *But that you may know that the Son of Man hath power upon the earth to forgive sins,...I say unto thee, Arise, take up thy couch, and go into thine house. And immediately he rose up before them, and took up that whereon he lay, and departed to his own house, glorifying God. And they were all amazed, and they glorified God* (Luke 5:24-26 KJV).

They laid my husband and me at God's feet, crying out for us to conceive and have a child. Their community of faith drew on the power of a risen Savior. They spoke and believed in the Word of God, giving Him all the reasons we should have a baby. Tears streamed down my face as I felt the fervency of their compassion, love, and empathy. This was certainly a different kind of meeting than I'd ever attended!

> *You younger people, submit yourselves to your elders. Yes, all of you be submissive to one another, and be clothed with humility, for "God resists the proud, but gives grace to the humble." Therefore, humble yourselves under the mighty hand of God, that He may exalt you in due time, casting all your care upon Him, for He cares for you* (1 Peter 5:5-7 NKJV).

As they prayed, even MY faith increased. I began to believe again. *If any of you lacks wisdom, let him ask of God, who gives to all liberally and without reproach, and it will be given to him. But let him ask in faith, with no doubting, for he who doubts is like a wave of the sea driven and tossed by the wind. For let not that man suppose that he will receive anything from the Lord; he is a double-minded man, unstable in all his ways* (James 1:5-8 NKJV).

Their faith bolstered my faith. I began to believe this was possible. God is bigger than anything. Miracles don't happen because of us but because we have a GOD of power. He absolutely loves and cares about us. When we suffer, He feels our pain. He is a God of compassion!

> *So the Lord said, "If you have faith as a mustard seed, you can say to this mulberry tree, 'Be pulled up by the roots and be planted in the sea,' and it would obey you"* (Luke 17:6 NKJV).

I began to believe God could and would do this—even if my past prevented me from loving myself completely. God is bigger than our sins and our past all put together. I knew I didn't deserve it, but His grace covered me. He deserved to be glorified through my life. It had nothing to do with me. It had everything to do with Him!

Four months later, I became pregnant! It wasn't without difficulty and required bedrest, but our baby grew to full term.

After only one contraction and just before the baby entered the birth canal, she flipped from being in a head-first position to being doubled over and backward. In that position, she broke my tailbone on the way out. But the excruciating pain was worth it to bring our beautiful, precious baby girl into the world. A perfect, wee, fair-haired baby girl with piercing, hazel, copper-flecked brown eyes. Truly, a MIRACLE BABY!

GOD IS FAITHFUL TO HIS WORD and to the cries of His people.

The prayer of faith makes the sick person whole. *Is anyone among you sick? Let him call for the elders of the church, and let them pray over him, anointing him with oil in the name of the Lord. And the prayer of faith will save the sick, and the Lord will raise him up. And if he has committed sins, he will be forgiven* (James 5:14-15 NKJV).

> *Confess your trespasses to one another and pray for one another, that you may be healed. The effective, fervent prayer of a righteous man avails much* (James 5:16 NKJV).

You see, these people who prayed did not speak negatively, nor did they gossip and fill the spiritual or physical atmospheres with curses, doubts, unbelief, or even negative beliefs. We must guard our hearts from negativities and doubt.

> *So above all, guard the affections of your heart, for they affect all that you are. Pay attention to the welfare of your innermost being, for from there flows the wellspring of life* (Proverbs 4:23 TPT).

I had to keep my heart believing, not looking at my circumstances, but looking instead to what God promised. *Give attention to my words; Incline your ear to my sayings. Do not let them depart from your eyes; Keep them in the midst of your heart; For they are life to those who find them and health to all their flesh* (Proverbs 4:20-22 NKJV).

I had to keep agreeing, and keep my words lining up with what God says, speaking words of life and not words of death.

> *Death and life are in the power of the tongue, And those who love it will eat its fruit* (Proverbs 18:21 NKJV).

Sometimes we just need to get desperate before we finally can trust others to cry out for us. In fact, when we are desperate enough, perhaps we are finally humble enough to receive a miracle. When we are desperate, we have an opportunity to cry out for ourselves—again and again. He hears us, and He makes Himself known to us through His power in ways we may have never known before. *When holy lovers of God cry out to Him with all their hearts, the Lord will hear them and come to rescue them from all their troubles. The Lord is close to all whose hearts are crushed by pain, and He is always ready to restore the repentant one* (Psalm 34:17-18 TPT).

The Word of God is true and will accomplish all it is sent to do.

> *So shall My word be that goes forth from My mouth; it shall not return to Me void, but it will accomplish what I please, and it shall prosper in the thing for which I sent it* (Isaiah 55:11 NKJV).

Oh, how wonderful to experience such a gift after having been barren for ten years! God restores barrenness into fruitfulness. *He grants the barren woman a home, like a joyful mother of children. Praise the Lord!* (Psalm 113:9 NKJV).

"For I will look on you favorably and make you fruitful, multiply you and confirm my covenant with you" (Leviticus 26:9 NKJV).

Five months later, to my total shock and amazement, I was pregnant again with my second miracle baby!

What? Really?

"I think I'm pregnant?" I told my husband with a question in my voice. "Could this be?"

My husband was surprised as well, "What?!"

Our wee babe was only five months old, and here I was, pregnant again!!!

God was giving me more than I could have ever asked, dreamed, or imagined!

Now to Him who is able to do exceedingly abundantly above all that we ask or think, according to the power that works in us (Ephesians 3:20 NKJV).

There must have been lots of power still working in and through me. His power works in us!

This time, my pregnancy was easy, which was good because I was far too busy running after our first child. The birth was smooth; from start to finish, it was just three hours of labour with only three pushes, and our second beautiful baby girl was born—this time with thick black hair. Her big, chocolate-brown eyes stared up at me. Wow! Our God is a miracle-working God!

> *Every good gift and every perfect gift is from above, and comes down from the Father of lights, with Whom there is no variation or shadow of turning. Of His own will He brought us forth by the word of truth, that we might be a kind of firstfruits of His creatures* (James 1:17-18 NKJV).

Years have passed, and these girls are beautiful inside and out—gorgeous to look at but also caring, compassionate, thoughtful, and giving. They are a blessing to all who know them. My eldest daughter and her husband now have four children: ages 16, 14, and 11 years, and recently, the youngest just turned seven months. My youngest daughter and her husband have five children: ages 14, 12, 11, 9, and 7 years old.

Besides my own children and grandchildren, I also share four stepchildren, their spouses, and their five children. I am a mother to eight and a grandmother to fourteen grandchildren! My heart overflows with thanksgiving and gratitude for my God, who not only hears but also answers prayer! He truly is a miracle-working God! *To Him be glory in the church by Christ Jesus to all generations, forever and ever. Amen* (Ephesians 3:21 NKJV).

THE MIRACLE OF PRAYER

by Kelley Rene

Prayer has been an integral part of my life for as long as I can remember. My mom was a prayer warrior, and she ensured her children prayed regularly and understood its power.

Jesus modeled prayer for us in the Bible and even demonstrated how we should pray in the now-famous "Lord's Prayer." *Our Father in heaven, Hallowed be Your name. Your kingdom come. Your will be done On earth, as it is in heaven. Give us this day our daily bread. And forgive us our debts, As we forgive our debtors. And do not lead us into temptation, but deliver us from the evil one. For Yours is the kingdom, and the power, and the glory forever. Amen* (Matthew 6:9-13 NKJV).

Throughout God's Word, we see the desperate, the lonely, the needy, the sick, and the unholy reach out to God in prayer. They pray with eloquence. In simplicity. Or even without using words. It doesn't matter the style. God's biggest desire is to have a relationship with us, and prayer offers us a direct line of communication with Him.

Don't worry about anything; instead pray about everything. Tell God what you need, and thank him for all he has done. Then you will experience God's peace, which exceeds anything we can understand. His peace will guard your hearts and minds as you live in Christ Jesus (Philippians 4:6-7 NLT).

When we're celebrating, we can offer God thanks through prayer. When we're lonely, we can ask for comfort. When we're experiencing pain, going through a difficult time, or struggling, we can call on Him. Whatever our need or situation, God is ready and willing to minister to us.

If you have a difficult time finding the right words to pray, first understand that there are no right or wrong words to pray. But one method that works for me is to restate scripture into a prayer. For example, you can pray Philippians 4:6-7 this way: *Lord, Your Word tells me not to worry about anything. I thank you for all you've done for me. I believe You care about me and my needs. Please give me peace in the area of ...* then share your trouble, need, or concern with Him—just like you're talking to a friend.

God wants to offer you comfort; He wants to give you peace. He will settle your nerves and guide and direct you—if only you ask. His wisdom is available to you with a simple request. He will answer. If Jesus prayed in His hours of need, how much more should we?

Colossians 4:2 says, *Continue steadfastly in prayer, being watchful in it with thanksgiving* (ESV).

I learned to pray at an early age, and it is how I survived numerous crises in my life. Even throughout the writing of this book, I sought God's assistance. We prayed God would send the very writers He desired to tell their stories within its pages. We asked God to impart into us the very words He wanted included. We asked Him to lead and guide us, squelch our fear and doubts. He responded in miraculous ways that amazed me at times. The more we seek Him, the more He reveals Himself to us.

Prayer should be our first reaction to our concerns and problems, not the last reaction when we've already made a bigger mess of the situation. Prayer is our direct connection to God. It is the way to build a relationship with Him. It's a way to show Him gratitude for all He's done in our lives. It's the way we submit our wills to Him.

> *"For I know the plans I have for you,"* says the Lord. *"They are plans for good and not disaster, to give you a future and a hope. In those days when you pray, I will listen"* (Jeremiah 29: 11-12 NLT).

When we humble ourselves and pray, God comes to our aid. He provides for our needs. He changes hearts and makes a way when, often, there seems to be no other way.

In order to have a Miracle Mindset, we must make prayer an everyday occurrence. When you wake up in the morning, praise God for a new day. When you go to bed at night, thank Him for keeping you safe, leading and directing your day, providing for your family, and any other way He has served you.

Remember: *Always be joyful. Never stop praying. Be thankful in all circumstances, for this is God's will for you who belong to Christ Jesus* (1 Thessalonians 5:16-18 NLT).

. . . .

LEECY BARNETT

Originally from Milwaukee, Wisconsin, Leecy Barnett has lived in Boynton Beach, Florida, for more than 30 years. Education has always been important to Leecy, who has a BA in history from Duke University, an MA in church history from Trinity Evangelical Divinity School, and an MA in Library Science from the University of South Florida. Although she never married nor had children, Leecy considers being a part of God's forever family for 50+ years a wonderful adventure.

Leecy's first career was in Christian ministry, focusing on college students from America as well as students and scholars from China. After she moved to Florida, Leecy began a second career as a librarian. However, she never stopped her involvement in ministry, teaching the Bible and writing for her church.

Leecy writes a column for Women World Leaders' *Voice of Truth* magazine, *Power Points: God at Work through Women Leaders Yesterday and Today.* She is also the author of two books: *Everything New (a Bible study for new believers) and Ten Life Lessons Worth Learning Over and Over Again.* For fun, Leecy enjoys reading, crafts, games, movies, Korean dramas, British television, and cheering on the Duke basketball team.

ORDINARY MIRACLES

By Leecy Barnett

A miracle is defined as "an extraordinary and astonishing happening that is attributed to the presence and action of an ultimate or divine power."[1] When I think of miracles in the Bible, I think of the spectacular ones: the parting of the Red Sea, Daniel in the lion's den, the feeding of the five thousand, and the resurrection of Jesus. Clearly, these were extraordinary and astonishing events; everyone who heard of them was amazed, thinking, *Wow, that is unbelievable!* But I contend that there are what I would call *ordinary* miracles—situations that require the intervention of God but are usually not seen as extraordinary and astonishing—although maybe they should be. Salvation, "deliverance from the power and effects of sin,"[2] is one such *ordinary miracle.* Because we say, "I received Christ" or "I decided to follow Jesus," it can seem that our spiritual life begins and ends with us. But Jesus said, *"Very truly I tell you, no one can enter the kingdom of God unless they are born of water and the Spirit," and "No one can come to me unless the Father who sent me draws them"* (John 3:5, 6:44a NIV). From first to last, coming to know the Father is an act of God. All this to say, my miracle mindset centers on the *ordinary miracle* of salvation—mine and my dad's.

In some ways, although we belong to the same family, my dad and I grew up in very different worlds.

Dad was a child of the Great Depression; in fact, he experienced it earlier than most of the country. The Depression hit farming communities, like the one Dad was born in, immediately after World War I. By the mid-1920s, my grandfather's farm equipment business went bust. During this same period, my father also lost his older brother, who suffered a tragic accident and subsequent infection. My grandfather never recovered from the death of his oldest son and tried to compensate by drinking and gambling. When the family moved from their small town to the big city of Madison, Wisconsin, my grandmother became the primary breadwinner as she owned and operated a boarding house that catered to students at the University of Wisconsin (UW). During those boarding house years, Dad never had his own bedroom and slept in whatever bed was available. Despite the hardship, he endured—working his way through UW and, after graduation, serving as an Army Aircorp pilot in World War II. The GI Bill enabled Dad to get both an accounting and law degree. With a little help from the government, he pulled himself up by his bootstraps and became a self-made man. Dad made it on his own and didn't see any need for a Savior.

I, on the other hand, was born smack dab in the middle of the Baby Boom generation. Thanks to my father's hard work, I grew up in a comfortable, middle-class suburb of Milwaukee. I never had to worry about money, and most of the problems I was aware of in my early childhood seemed like the *Leave it to Beaver* or *Father Knows Best* type—nothing earthshaking.

But Dad and I did have one thing in common. We both grew up going to church just because it was a good and socially acceptable thing to do. My mom had become a Jesus follower as a young girl, and her faith meant a lot to her. But her home church was way too conservative and legalistic for my dad, so they compromised and found a local church they could attend together. As a result, I grew up in a liberal Baptist denomination, and I thought Christianity was mostly about being good and avoiding certain bad things. For example, as a part of our church covenant, we pledged to abstain from drinking alcohol. If they ever talked about the good news that Jesus died and rose again so that we could be forgiven and know God personally, I completely missed it.

I don't know what Dad thought, but to my understanding, I could work my way into heaven by being good. And when I looked around, I figured I was a much better person than most people. My self-righteousness and spiritual pride kept me from knowing God because, deep down, I felt I didn't need His help.

By the time I was a senior in high school, the *Jesus Movement* was in full swing, and I couldn't help bumping into it from time to time. When our church youth group went on a retreat at the Green Lake Conference Center, there was also an enthusiastic group of college Jesus people there. One of the guys came up and asked me if I "knew Jesus." I blew him off. I thought I already "knew Jesus," whatever that meant. One of the girls in my high school class brought a Bible to school every day, and everyone labeled her a Jesus freak. I saw a documentary on TV about young people in California and other places around the country turning to Jesus. I remember thinking, *I wish I had their faith.* Since my curiosity was peaked, I wrote a term paper for my English composition class on the Jesus movement. I clearly had an academic interest in Jesus, but it never touched my heart. That would require admitting I couldn't handle life on my own— that I was a sinner and needed saving.

Dad was always a great advocate for education in his children's lives. Therefore, one of the highlights of our father-daughter relationship was a trip to visit the three colleges I had applied to in Ohio, New York, and North Carolina. I chose to go to Duke because it was academically challenging and, located in North Carolina, promised much better weather than I experienced in my native Wisconsin. Also, I knew it was secretly my dad's favorite because he had been really impressed with the library when we visited. However, he was determined not to say which college he favored, so the choice was all my own.

Duke was founded as a Methodist school, so there is a massive chapel in the center of the campus, the logical place for me to attend Sunday services. I tried out for the chapel choir but didn't make the cut because I couldn't sight-read music. I continued to go but became uncomfortable when they prayed the Lord's prayer. As Methodists, they used the words "forgive us our trespasses," and I, a Baptist, said, "forgive us our debts." So, I stopped attending chapel. (It is amazing what trivial excuses we come up with to keep us from worshipping God!) Instead, I vowed to find a church in town, which I never did. Out of laziness, I let my habit of church attendance drop. I honestly didn't miss it much—because Christianity was just a religion to me, worship was only a duty, and I knew I could keep being good enough all on my own.

During my freshman year, the most popular movie was *The Godfather*. My boyfriend Bill and I decided to see it together on, of all days, Good Friday. During the pivotal scene where Michael Corleone is in church making vows to become the godfather to his sister's baby, the priest asks Michael if he believes in God the Father, Jesus Christ, and the Holy Ghost. The film kept cutting to scenes of the Corleone family assassinating their rivals on Michael's orders. Michael knew all the right answers, and in his proud and perverted heart, he thought his life was pleasing to God. At the end of the movie, I cried uncontrollably. When Bill asked me what was wrong, I blurted out, "I don't know if I believe in God anymore." My confession shocked me. I had always been religious and never doubted God's existence, but I saw myself in Michael Corleone. I knew all the right answers and thought my self-righteousness gave me favor with God, but true faith had no place in my heart. Michael and I were both hypocrites, not true believers.

The very next day, my parents arrived for a visit, and we attended chapel together on Easter Sunday. Dad was very moved by the service, during which they played part of Mahler's "Resurrection" Symphony, which he absolutely loved. For me, however, the worship only served to point out how far I was from God and how empty my life had become. On Monday, as I boarded the intercampus bus, I spotted my good friend, Bev, who was on her way to a Bible study. I had never heard of people studying the Bible outside of a church—I was intrigued. I was eager to meet people who genuinely believed in God, and I invited myself to the study. The women I met there talked about having a personal relationship with Jesus Christ. Suzie, the group leader, said that on Easter morning she and her boyfriend went for a walk and prayed together. I was amazed because praying was the last thing my boyfriend would ever do with me. Then Suzie gave me a booklet that explained the difference between knowing about God and knowing Him *personally*.

I took the booklet back to my dorm and read it while I took a bath (lest my roommate think I was a Jesus freak). One Bible verse caught my attention, *For by grace you have been saved through faith; and this is not of yourselves, it is the gift of God; not a result of works, so that no one may boast* (Ephesians 2:8-9 NASB). Grace was the complete opposite of my do-it-yourself religion. According to the Bible, I would never be *good enough* on my own. Faith in what Jesus had done for me was the key. I knew I didn't have faith, and I wasn't sure how to get it.

A couple of weeks later, what was supposed to be the best weekend of our college experience, ended up with me sitting in my dorm room—alone. Bill had gone to the beach with his buddies during Joe College Weekend, which left me without a date. On that Sunday, I decided to get out and visit the local church Suzie and Bev recommended. I could sense a difference in this congregation. There was a spirit of love that permeated the church building. When the pastor invited us to kneel in prayer, I knew I wanted what they had. Still full of doubts, I asked Jesus to come into my life and change it with His love. Amazingly, He did. It wasn't because I was a good person or had great faith; it was, as the Bible verse said, a true gift from God: freely given, no strings attached. Even having faith to believe He would give me this gift was not something I had to work up to; God gave me faith when I desperately wanted and needed it.

Ironically, at the same time my faith was coming alive, Dad was giving up all pretext of being a believer in Christ. The summer after my freshman year in college, my parents moved about 30 minutes across town. The distance made it impractical for us to continue attending the church we belonged to during my early years. Mom found a church in our new neighborhood, but Dad stopped going to church altogether. He never explained why, but I can speculate about his reasons. First, he figured three of his four children were grown up and out of the house, and my younger brother was a high school sophomore—practically an adult. I believe Dad's main goal in attending church was to give his children a moral foundation, and he felt he had achieved that goal. Secondly, since Dad believed, as I had, that Christianity is mostly about doing good, he figured he could do good on his own without help from religion. Dad was big on civic engagement. He was active in the Boy Scouts and the Boys and Girls Clubs and was the chair of the fundraising committee for the Milwaukee United Performing Arts Fund. If good deeds could get you into heaven, Dad must have felt he had a good chance of making the cut.

Still, Dad seemed to take my new faith in stride. My being a Jesus follower was fine with him as long as I was happy and didn't try to convert him. He was a very private person who never talked about his feelings or what mattered most deeply to him. For the first ten years of my faith journey, Dad continued to be supportive of my choices—including going into full-time ministry after graduation and spending two years serving halfway around the world preaching to students in Guam, Micronesia, and the Philippines. When I returned from the Far East in 1981, I learned Dad had been diagnosed with prostate cancer. Even this disease did not seem to depress my optimistic father. While undergoing radiation treatments, he joked with the technologists and offered to pay them a dollar for each new expression they could come up with to tell him to scoot down the exam table.

Fortunately, Dad went into remission for the next nine years and was able to see the birth of six of his seven grandchildren. Then in 1990, he had quadruple bypass surgery. Less than a year later, his cancer was back. This time the prognosis discouraged my typically confident father.

One Sunday, not long after he received the cancer news, Dad got dressed, not in his usual golf outfit, but in a suit, and announced to Mom that he was going to church with her. After a twenty-year absence from church, Dad obviously had eternally significant concerns on his mind. I believe he knew he couldn't fight cancer on his own and needed some divine intervention.

At about this time, I was feeling restless in my ministry position and sensed God leading me to make a change, so I accepted a teaching position in a Christian high school in South Florida. The school was located close to Boynton Beach, where my parents had a winter home for more than a decade. I began teaching in August of 1991, and my parents came down for the *season* a couple of months later. My father, whom I had seen only three months before, had become so frail. Mom was worried because his appetite was gone; the only food he wanted to eat was his childhood favorite, graham crackers in milk. Despite his frailty, my father rallied and shared his experiences in World War II with my American history class. That was to be one of his last significant outings.

A month after arriving for his winter stay in Florida, it became clear Dad was in the final stages of life. When hospice came to prepare my parents' home for Dad's last days, I decided it was now or never to talk with him about Jesus. I joined him in his study, a favorite retreat where he spent hours doing his favorite pastimes—reading and listening to classical music. After years of praying for Dad and finding him completely closed off to spiritual things, I asked if I could read the Bible to him. I was surprised when he gave his consent. I opened to the gospel of John.

"Do not let your hearts be troubled. You believe in God; believe also in me. My Father's house has many rooms; if that were not so, would I have told you that I am going there to prepare a place for you? And if I go and prepare a place for you, I will come back and take you to be with me that you may also be where I am. You know the way to the place where I am going."

Thomas said to him, "Lord, we don't know where you are going, so how can we know the way?"

Jesus answered, "I am the way and the truth and the life. No one comes to the Father except through me. If you really know me, you will know my Father as well. From now on, you do know him and have seen him."
(John 14: 1-7 NIV)

After I finished, I asked Dad if I could pray with him. Again, he said, "Yes." To me, this seemed extraordinary and astonishing. My dad was admitting that he needed something outside of himself; he needed God. This very proud and self-sufficient man was humbling himself before almighty God. I prayed aloud, and Dad prayed silently. I knew God had done a miraculous work in my dad's heart.

The very next day, Dad went dramatically downhill, and Mom felt she could not care for him at home as planned. She thought he would die at any moment. So she called for an ambulance which rushed him to the inpatient hospice facility. Miraculously, Dad perked up and was lucid enough to experience goodbye visits from my siblings. Right after, Dad slipped into a coma. He died a few days later.

Perhaps you, like my dad and I used to, think Christianity is mostly about being good and avoiding certain bad things. You may believe your good works are *good enough* to make you acceptable to God. But the Bible teaches, *"No one is righteous—not even one. No one is truly wise; no one is seeking God"...For everyone has sinned; we all fall short of God's glorious standard* (Romans 3:10-11, 23 NLT). I know this can be a hard pill to swallow if you have always considered yourself a good person. But the very next verse tells us the good news: *Yet God, in his grace, freely makes us right in his sight. He did this through Christ Jesus when he freed us from the penalty for our sins* (Romans 3:24 NLT). If you humble yourself, the *ordinary miracle* of God's grace, His unearned acceptance, is available to you. Stop relying on your own efforts to win God's approval, and trust in what Jesus did to free us from the performance trap. That is the miracle of salvation.

[1]Werblowsky, R. Z. (2018, July 23). Miracle. *Encyclopedia Britannica.* https://www.britannica.com/topic/miracle

[2]Merriam-Webster. (n.d.). Salvation. In *Merriam-Webster.com dictionary.* Retrieved March 3, 2020, from https://www.merriam-webster.com/dictionary/salvation

THE MIRACLE OF SALVATION

by Julie T. Jenkins

The biggest miracle God offers us is, without a doubt, the miracle of salvation.

Our perfect, holy God created us to live in paradise with Him forever. And it was going swimmingly—for a short period of time. But then mankind, being imperfect, sinned, setting all of humanity apart from God.

You see, our God is so holy that nothing that is not holy can reside in His presence. It is a physical impossibility.

But God knows us so well that He understood we would sin and create this chasm between Him and us, so He made a way for us to cross that chasm.

God sent His own Son, Jesus, to earth to live in full humanity. Jesus was born like any other baby—helpless and needy. His parents cared for Him, and He grew, learning first-hand the ways of the world. As He grew physically, the Spirit also awakened within Him, giving Him wisdom of His heavenly Father as He prayed and studied scripture. Jesus worked, learned, and matured. But one thing He never did was sin. Jesus never sinned against God or against any other human. He did what no human could do before or after Him: He remained holy. Sinless.

This is important because the penalty for sin is death—eternal separation from our heavenly Father. But Jesus never sinned. So He should have never been separated from God.

And yet, as the Bible and history both teach us, Jesus did die. In fact, He was killed. He was crucified on a cross for all the world to witness—kind of an "I told you so" moment for those who had risen up against Jesus' teachings that He was the Son of God.

But it was all for the miracle of salvation! Jesus' death was all part of God's plan.

Jesus was born on earth as a man so He could die for our sins.

When we sin, we separate ourselves from the holiness of God. That is the penalty of sin. But when perfect and holy Jesus CHOSE to die, He did so to pay that penalty for OUR sins—so we wouldn't ever have to die. So we could spend eternity in heaven with God the Father.

Jesus CHOSE the agony of being separated from God so we wouldn't have to.

And after three days of being separated from God, Jesus rose from the dead—our debt paid and His glory restored.

That is the miracle of salvation!

And although our salvation hinges on God's love and Jesus' commitment to us, it does not occur without our cooperation.

In order to actualize our salvation, we must willingly choose to accept the gift Jesus offers us.

When I was a kid, one non-negotiable in our home was that if we received a gift, we had to write a thank you note. We had to acknowledge the gift personally, graciously thanking the giver. Then we had to put a stamp on the envelope and mail it. Only then could we use or enjoy the gift. There were no exceptions to this rule.

And there are no exceptions with God.

To receive the miracle of salvation, we must acknowledge the receipt of this awesome gift. We must personally thank Jesus as the only One who is able to offer us this gift. When we do, He will infuse us with His Holy Spirit, allowing us free access to use and enjoy our salvation, our unbreakable re-union with God, for eternity.

The miracle of salvation is wholly dependent on Jesus, but we must graciously thank our Giver for the transaction to be complete.

If you have not yet experienced the miracle of salvation, I invite you to pray with me now:

Dear Heavenly Father, thank you for your miracle of salvation! Thank you for always keeping me in your sights, even when I've knowingly sinned against you. God, I turn my face to you. I ask for your forgiveness, and I accept the gift of salvation that only you can offer me. Jesus, thank you for dying for me to pay for my sins. Thank you for giving up your place in heaven to come to earth and live a sinless life, enduring the temptations of the flesh, the world, and the devil so that you could pay MY debt of sin. Holy Spirit, thank you for entering into my life now. Thank you for the wisdom and guidance you promise to impart as I walk through this life. I promise not to take this gift lightly! And when I mess up, God, I will turn back to you, knowing you will never turn away from me. Empower me to be all that you have called me to be. In Jesus' name, I pray. Amen.

· ·

MELISSA GISSY WITHERSPOON

After more than two decades of substance abuse, Melissa Gissy Witherspoon has finally achieved long-term sobriety and is eager to share with the world that recovery from substance use disorder is possible! *With God all things are possible* (Matthew 19:26 NIV).

Originally from a suburb north of Atlanta, Georgia, Melissa currently resides in Winston-Salem, North Carolina, where she is raising her youngest of four children with her husband, Derek. With a decade in sobriety, she is following her calling to love and support those whose lives have been impacted by addiction. As founder and CEO of Sober-Now, Melissa raises proceeds from her best-selling, award-winning book, *I'm Sober...So Now What? A Journey of Hope and Healing,* to bring hope to prison ministries, recovery centers, sober-living housing, churches, and high schools.

When Melissa is not working as an administrative assistant at church, you will find her advocating for the recovery community, sharing her story of God's love through podcasts, speaking events, recovery walks, supporting accountability courts, and offering inspiration through her social media pages.

Some of Melissa's accolades include: 2022 International Book Awards Finalist, 2023 BookFest Award Addiction and Recovery, 2023 BookFest Award Self Help-Inspiration, and NY Times Square BookFest Bilboard Montague.

You can connect with Melissa at Melissa@Sober-Now.com or www.Linktr.ree/sobernow

God's Grace and Mercy, One Day at a Time

by Melissa Gissy Witherspoon

Therefore do not worry about tomorrow, for tomorrow will worry about itself. Each day has enough trouble of its own (Matthew 6:34 NIV).

"I bet you all are wondering why I've called you to this meeting..."

This is how I started most of my business ventures or training events in my property management career. With every God-given strand of curly hair blown-out silky smooth, eyelashes and lips painted on just so, a tailored business suit—black, of course, and pressed at every seam, I'd stand before my team, appearing as if I had my entire act together.

Inside, I would chant to myself a series of movements—robotic in my brain. But on the outside, I exuded charisma and charm.

Shoulders back and chin up, Melissa. Take deep breaths but not too deep—you don't want them to smell that you've had wine and cigarettes for breakfast, do you? Look them straight in the forehead. If you stare into their eyes, they will know you are a fraud.

Now say something funny and slightly cute to gain the men's attention. Flip your hair, but follow up with a serious fact as if you are prepared. Make sure to relate it to one of the women in the room—you'll want them on your side, too. Quick...pause as if you are thinking deeply about the topic and ask an open-ended question. Hurry up! They are glaring at you as if they know you are still drunk.

Oh good...you saved yourself this time, Missy. You are sure to snatch that promotion right out from under Mrs. Fancy-Pants over there! Tell them you will circle back around to them and exit out of here while you are still ahead of the game. You deserve a nice alcoholic beverage on the way home to reward yourself for barely pulling that one off! While you are at it, you might as well pop some more Xanax. After all, you are going to need strength to make it through the night of playing happy wife and present-mother when you get home, right?

These actual thoughts ran through my brain, day in and day out. *Can you imagine?* It was an exhausting game of trying to keep up and appear functional while maintaining a comfortable numb, using drugs and alcohol in copious amounts. And that is just a small example of what my career life looked like. That doesn't even touch my romantic relationships or interactions with my children and other family members. And don't get me started on trying to juggle *friends*—most of whom were just drinking associates.

My life was comprised of an ongoing series of lies and attempts to connect the dots of manufactured stories I obviously couldn't keep up with because I was so inebriated most of the time. I began my days by funneling through text messages from the night before and lining up bar receipts, trying to put all the pieces together. My days usually ended with me passed out, face down on the floor somewhere. This went on for years and years. Twenty-three years, to be exact.

How did I get there? How did I go from the happy home where my loving parents raised my two precious siblings and me to attempting to take my own life on the floor of my unfinished basement twenty-plus years later?

My spiral began in my teen years—when I found myself running with the wrong crowd. So desperate for approval and acceptance, I basically sold my soul to the devil to get the attention I craved. It wasn't long afterward I found myself living in a drug dealer's home, being used to entertain clients against my will. In just a few short months, my life had changed forever. With my innocence ripped away and my trust in men voided, I moved through the next twenty-plus years trying to mask the emotional pain that filled me from that experience rather than working through it.

My addiction didn't evolve overnight. I didn't just wake up one day and say, "I think I'll be an alcoholic today." Much like how cancer grows, it slowly took over and consumed me. I cultivated and appropriated my disease of addiction over time. All of the elements needed to make my addiction thrive were there. A family history of substance abuse, guilt, shame, self-doubt, failure, loss of connection, lack of spirituality, and a growing need for instant gratification all worked together to propel me down the rabbit hole of chasing the next high.

I traded morals and integrity for shortcuts and an *I'll-get-them-before-they-get-me* mentality. Sure, it was my choice to do all these things. My own free will led me there. But many factors over the years and my lack of reasonable cognitive thinking from a very early age helped contribute to my poor decision-making. At some point along the way, without even realizing it, my brain chemistry changed, and my substance use turned to substance abuse, also known as the disease of addiction.

Eventually, the devastating path I chose led me to my rock bottom with drugs and alcohol. And that rock bottom delivered me to the cold, hard floor of my unfinished basement, where I attempted to leave this world well before I was meant to. I just couldn't find the strength to endure one more day as an alcoholic and drug addict. I couldn't, for one more minute, look into the eyes of those I cared for and see the pain I was causing them.

Nothing worked to rid me of my obsession—not the months of inpatient and outpatient treatment, hours of counseling, or revolving doors of incarceration for drinking and driving. I was left seemingly unfazed by the ongoing trauma of multiple failed marriages, job loss after job loss, drained bank accounts, car wrecks, and family and friends who just couldn't stand to be around me anymore. Multiple abusive relationships ending with restraining orders and court battles had no effect on me. Even losing my own children was not enough to break the chains of addiction holding me captive. None of it shook me enough to loosen the grip of my fingers around my precious prize in a bottle marked "Vodka."

Each attempt to cure me of the terrible disease of addiction ended in complete failure, perpetuating yet another cycle of binge drinking to mask the shame of not having the capability of being *normal*. Relapsing from my substance abuse "recovery" became a redundant part of my battle, and I saw no way of jumping off the hamster wheel. That is until the day I found myself on the unfinished floor of my basement, waiting for my inevitable trip to hell. That's exactly where I thought I would go the day I tried to take my own life. After all the havoc I had wreaked, where else could I expect to end up?

In the days leading up to my suicide attempt, I bantered questions back and forth in my head that I couldn't find answers to. *How could God allow such painful things to happen to me? And how could He ever love me for the choices I made through my painful experiences?* And because I'd lived so many years in guilt and shame, *How can God love me?* My victim mentality didn't allow me to go outside myself to find the answers to those tough questions. These thoughts perpetuated my cycle of insanity. *If there really was a God, how could He love me after all the shameful things I had done, and how could He forgive me for them?*

With a final note written, my house clean, and everything put in order so I could leave this world behind, I gobbled handfuls of pills I obtained from my recent trip to rehab, chased them down with my best bottle of vodka, cut my wrists, and laid there awaiting my fate. As I faded in and out, begging God to allow me to die, I saw a figure. It told me that if I would completely turn my will over to God, I would be free; I was supposed to be alive. It said I had a purpose to fulfill, which would all eventually make sense if I trusted my Creator, even when it felt impossible to do so.

It's hard to explain how these messages came to me. It wasn't as if you and I were having a conversation with each other; instead, they came from a voice deep inside of me. The figure talked to me, but the mouth didn't move. I felt a warm hug, and love shot through my entire body. Imagine being warmed from the inside out and feeling no pain—just a calm, steady flow of energy and love. It was the most intense feeling of love I have ever felt.

Soon after, my husband came home and found me. I was granted a new lease on life. I took the opportunity and gave one last try at a long-term inpatient dual-diagnosis treatment facility, and I never looked back. That experience was the game changer in my attempt to recover from addiction.

The missing piece was that I hadn't previously had an authentic relationship with God. And every day moving forward from that point, I was determined to go to any length to find out how to make that happen.

You see, my friend, up until that moment, I had known of God, but I never truly knew Him. I was never in a committed relationship with Him. Okay, perhaps I was in a one-sided relationship, going to Him with calls for help to dig me out of whatever mess I had created and issuing desperate infrequent pleas for Him to rescue me—with no reciprocation of love or respect. But that had been the extent of my prayer life: begging for His grace and emptily promising to change, all while having no actual intent to adjust any behavior.

How could you really blame me? I had no genuine concept of love, much less any understanding of unconditional love. I know now that God *is* love, but at the time, both God and love were foreign concepts to me. I certainly lacked respect for myself which impacted my ability to have respect for others, especially a God I wasn't even sure existed.

But our merciful Father found me lying on my basement floor almost lifeless, and, instead of walking away, He gently revealed to me a vision of grace and mercy. The vision I was granted was Divine. I believe He was responding to the prayers others had sent to Him. Those who had begged for His intercession when I could not had reached the heavens. And God rescued me in His perfect timing, allowing me to lean into Him as He healed my broken soul so I could one day bring a message of hope and healing to others. Just as Matthew 18:12-14 describes, God truly does leave the ninety-nine sheep for that one who wandered off. And now I am with the flock where I belong.

Now, I understand that God was there all along, through every bit of the messy, tangled web that had ensnared me. He was with me through my choices and circumstances that came from following my own will rather than His. Honestly, I had all but turned my back on Him. Yet His love, grace, and mercy pursued me. Sure, I am still wobbly in my faith. But over time, my relationship with our Creator has blossomed into a beautiful one, full of ebb and flow movements as His grace and mercy offer me courage and strength, one day at a time.

One of the most beautiful sayings I've learned in my recovery from addiction is "One day at a time." At first, I hated that phrase, but the truth in this simple statement borrowed from my 12-step recovery program, which has become a leading mantra for me, is that it's not just for those recovering from substance use disorders. It is for all of His people—every one of us.

A grace granted by our loving Father encourages us to stay in the present moment. It is easy to get so overwhelmed by the tasks and lists that fall into our laps. But the craziness and chaos of this world are not designed by our loving Father. Instead, these distractions are created by the accuser and carried out by us if we follow our own ego-driven wills rather than doing what God asks of us. The enemy who accuses God's children day and night (Revelation 12:10) loves nothing more than to pull us from the ability to connect with, be of service to, and love one another as Jesus has asked us to do. Drugs, alcohol, porn, food, gambling, lying, cheating, and stealing are self-serving distractions, the devil's shortcuts, if you will, meant to place a veil between us and a God who wants nothing more than for us to go to Him.

God desires that we stay connected with Him on an intimate level and receive His love so we may carry it back into this world filled with chaos and disorder. The devil thrives off of keeping us from having a steady, loving relationship with our Father. But if we stay in the moment, connected to God through prayer, meditation, and gratitude, we can create a safe place from the intentions of evil. We will see things clearly, without being overwhelmed, and become capable of being good stewards of faith, each moment, each day. Whatever is behind us and in front of us becomes less of a focus, and the present-day moment becomes a gift that can truly be filled with purpose.

I do not claim to be perfect in my faith. In fact, I wavered throughout the entire process of writing this chapter. Self-deprecating thoughts of *I'm not Christ-centered enough to write with the other authors. I can't recite Scripture the way they can and apply it to my stories in the way that they do. I'm just not good enough.* But maybe that's my part in this book. Maybe that's why God aligned it for us to connect right at this very moment—as a reminder that none of us are perfect.

We are all called to do hard, scary things we don't think are possible. I am sharing a piece of my story with prayers and hope that it stirs something in you—something that will inspire you to call on Him. Anyway, and anytime. God searched for me at my darkest hour and rescued me from the storm. He continues to grant me opportunities to share my story of faith with others. He will do the same for you! We are all His children, uniquely and perfectly made in His design. His love is infinite and abundant enough for us all.

God's love reminds me—a mother of four—of how deeply I love all my children. I would go to any length to support them and guide them. They are all so different from each other, yet I love them all the same. Unconditionally. I envision God our Father feeling the same way about each of us. He created us each in His image, with our own special purpose. To me, this alone is a miracle.

But for me, having a Miracle Mindset didn't just come from the resilience I learned through my slow, rigorous climb from the rock bottom of addiction. Instead, God gifted me with a Miracle Mindset as He spiritually awakened me—guiding me to give everything to Him and fully trust His will over mine. No mindset can be more powerful than that—a mindset centered by God. Our human mind is incapable of fully understanding the precise order He designed for this world. Giving myself over to His care will always be the biggest miracle for me.

I stumble all the time with keeping my ego in check, making sure what I do is for the greater glory rather than serving illusions and instant gratification. My recovery program taught me accountability, integrity, and how to serve others and function on life's terms without numbing the pain. It also taught me how to maneuver through each task or challenge and feel all the emotions that come with this gift of life.

But God. He is the one who grants me the grace, mercy, and unconditional love to endure it all. He never fails. I've tested His faith in me. Each time, He patiently waits for me to run back to Him as He guides me through situations each step of the way.

I may be the author of this chapter, but according to Hebrews 12:2 (ASV), Jesus is the author and perfecter of my faith and yours. As you move through life living out your own faith story, I encourage you to stay connected, love others, and keep moving forward bravely and boldly—even when things seem impossible. Embrace the Miracle Mindset of God's endless love and infinite grace and mercy. Until we meet again, know that you have a purpose, you are loved, and you are not alone on your journey. You are a miracle with a Miracle Mindset to do beautiful things in this gift of life, one day at a time.

For we are God's handiwork, created in Christ Jesus to do good works, which God prepared in advance for us to do (Ephesians 2:10 NIV).

FINDING THE MIRACLE IN DEFEAT

by Julie T. Jenkins

> Because of the Lord's great love we are not consumed,
> for his compassions never fail.
> They are new every morning;
> great is your faithfulness.
> (Lamentations 3:22-23 NIV)

When we read these verses written by the prophet Jeremiah, we see a picture of a man with a true Miracle Mindset. Jeremiah is the author of two books in the Bible. The first book, *Jeremiah,* predicts the destruction of Jerusalem; and in his second book, *Lamentations,* he responds to that destruction of his home.

Jeremiah understood the meaning of the word defeat.

I challenge you to read Lamentations. It is a vivid description of heartbreak and mourning—five chapters of literal crying out to God for mercy:

All her friends have betrayed her (1:2 NIV).
All who honored her despise her (1:8 NIV).
Her fall was astounding; there was none to comfort her (1:9 NIV).
My eyes fail from weeping, I am in torment within (2:11 NIV).
He has weighed me down with chains (3:7 NIV).
I have been deprived of peace (3:17 NIV).

Now that's a picture of defeat! Jeremiah suffered pain and heartbreak as the people of Jerusalem turned away from God. In fact, Jeremiah is known by many as "the weeping prophet" and says of himself:

I am the man who has seen affliction
by the rod of the Lord's wrath.
He has driven me away and made me walk
in darkness rather than light;
indeed, he has turned his hand against me
again and again, all day long (3:1-3 NIV).

But as we read the lament that pours forth from Jeremiah, we also see that God graced Jeremiah with the ability to look through the defeat to see an incredible miracle. Despite the defeat that was so apparent in his life, Jeremiah saw hope.

And despite any season of defeat we walk through, whether brought on by outside circumstances or even our own sin, as God's children, we will always have hope—because we will always be protected by God's love and compassion.

Because of the Lord's great love we are not consumed,
for his compassions never fail.
They are new every morning;
great is your faithfulness.
I say to myself, "The Lord is my portion;
therefore I will wait for him."
The Lord is good to those whose hope is in him,
to the one who seeks him;
it is good to wait quietly for the salvation of the Lord (3:22-26 NIV).

You see, once we give our lives to Christ, once we invite Him into our hearts to be our Lord and Savior, the miracle of His love will overwhelm us for the rest of our days.

Even when we feel defeated, we can look *through* our circumstances and see the miracle of God's love protecting us, guiding us, and giving us hope.

Reading through Lamentations, we see the real ebb and flow of pain and compassion, anger and love, defeat and hope. And that is what life feels like sometimes for us, too. I love that the Bible doesn't sugar-coat being a Christ-follower, which can be so difficult. But the Bible also reminds us that we must never forget we serve a God who will always listen to our cries. And we can trust that the God of all restoration will always bring beauty from our ashes in His perfect timing.

Because with God, the only lasting defeat is the defeat of evil.

When you feel defeat on your doorstep, child of God, simply turn away. Let God deal with the devil. And let Him shower you with His miracles of love, compassion, faithfulness, and hope. I guarantee you that our faithful God will never let you down.

. . . .

KIMBERLY EWELL

Kimberly Ewell has been walking with the Lord for eleven years. During that time, she learned to walk in faith and obedience, which brought her to where she is today. After years of healing and training, Kimberly founded WildFire International Ministries in Orlando, Florida, and has become a bestselling published author sharing her experiences and the love of God that changed her life forever.

Because of Kimberly's personal experiences of childhood trauma, abuse, pain, grief, and loss, Kimberly has been given a powerful testimony of God's love and healing power.

As part of Kimberly's journey, the Lord called her to Colorado Springs, CO., to learn ministry work at Focus on the Family. Here she gained experience of what it's like to be on the battlefield's front lines. The Lord opened Kimberly's eyes to the depths of the brokenness that runs rampant across the world. During her time at Focus on the Family, she ministered, counseled, and poured out the love of Jesus to many people across the nation.

Kimberly firmly believes that every person should be empowered to fulfill their God-given calling and destiny. She desires to see people healed and living in freedom.

Kimberly can be reached at wildfireintl.us@gmail.com

WHO I THINK I AM ISN'T WHO GOD SAYS I AM

by Kimberly Ewell

> *Finally, brethren, whatever things are true, whatever things are noble, whatever things are just, whatever things are pure, whatever things are lovely, whatever things are of good report, if there is any virtue and if there is anything praiseworthy— meditate on these things (Philippians 4:8 NKJV).*

As a child, I recall lying on a hillside with my eyes closed, feeling the blades from the tall, luscious green grass poking against my back. With my eyes closed, my senses were heightened to what was surrounding me on the hillside. The intense warmth from the sun's rays beat down on my face creating stillness in my body and causing my mind to become quiet. The gentle breeze brushed across me, and the leaves danced in the wind to the song of the birds. It was like being at a symphony—the trees and I were the audience listening to the birds singing beautiful melodies to one another.

Absorbing this moment, I opened my eyes to gaze upon the blue sky scattered with fluffy white clouds. My childlike mind began to create shapes of animals as the clouds moved across the sky into formation. A horse galloped across the heavens. Puffs of white clouds gathered to create what looked like mountains. My imagination made these images undeniably real.

As I lay there in the midst of having fun with the clouds, I questioned my existence. I knew God created me. And yet, I still wondered. *Why? Who am I?*

As we mature, we often ask life questions. From our season of childhood to our growth into teenagers and then adulthood, seeds are planted by people—our parents, friends, the enemy, and the things of this world.

For as he thinks in his heart, so is he (Proverbs 23:7 AMP).

Our reactions to these experiences, positive or negative, shape our minds and thoughts, thus developing our beliefs about ourselves, others, and God.

As a five-year-old girl, one of my negative experiences was being sexually assaulted several times by a neighbor.

The perpetrator mercilessly told me what he was about to do to me and then graphically foretold what he would do the next time. His words were very descriptive, and my innocent mind couldn't understand anything he said. I distinctly remember his warning, "Don't tell anyone, or you will be in trouble."

A bad seed was planted, and fear cropped up in my little mind. I began to water it by embracing the lies and believing his actions were my fault. This was the beginning of what would later be harvested in my life, causing me to question who I am.

How did I allow this to produce a negative harvest? It began when I embraced and believed all the lies. The more I focused on the negative words spoken over me and the negative thoughts and visions, the more I became the person God never intended me to be. My name changed from Kimberly—the happy, laughing, trusting, bubbly little girl, to "No Name"—a shameful, disgusting, guilty, dirty, and cautious little girl. I lost who God created me to be, and as I grew up, I became a very damaged person. I completely lost my identity!

What happened to me was not of God. It was from the enemy who came to steal, kill, and destroy me. Young children are his most prominent target. Satan wants to corrupt our minds at the earliest possible age. Why? I believe there are a couple of reasons. First, Satan does not want us to have the slightest relationship with the Lord. Second, he is after our identity and doesn't want us to know who we are in Christ Jesus.

Many other negative occurrences transpired in my life over the years, causing me to continue to be deceived about my identity. One occurred when I was nine years old and lived in Washington state.

I was playing in the woods with my brother and two of our friends who were brothers. I loved running through the tall fir trees and leaping over the massive, hollow, old logs. We crawled through the logs, not thinking twice about the bugs or other critters occupying those dark, musty spaces.

Hours later, after some huffing and puffing, we were exhausted and needed something to drink. As we took a break, David, one of the two boys we played with, said to me, "You're pretty."

I was shy and turned my head and smiled, feeling a bit embarrassed at the same time.

Then, in the midst of flattery, he immediately followed the compliment with, "You're pretty... UGLY!" and laughed.

I was crushed! His words triggered all the lies spoken to me when I was younger and birthed yet another lie from the pit. From that day forward, I watered every negative seed spoken over me. I believed all those hurtful words.

I was ugly.

Every bad thing in my life was my fault.

Guilt grew within me even when I knew I had done nothing wrong.

And I believed compliments offered to me were lies or obligatory niceties.

Over the years, I'd hear voices telling me how fat I was, that I was ugly and not good enough, no one loved me, and my body wasn't perfect. At thirteen, I took over-the-counter diet pills and used Sun In hair lightener or fresh lemons to change my brown hair to blond. Because of my insecurity, I thought this would make me attractive and cause people to like me; and then maybe I'd like myself too.

Despite my efforts, I still struggled with who I was. I didn't like what I saw in the mirror, and all the while, the negative thoughts continued. I became what I thought I was.

You're so ugly! You're so fat. Something is wrong with you!

I listened to a broken record!

As a young adult, I sought help to overcome the traumas in my life. I saw a psychologist and went to secular and church counselors. But no one could help me. The only one who could help was someone I didn't yet know.

Jesus.

Then, just fifteen years ago, at 43 years old, I was overcome with unhappiness with how I looked after breastfeeding five babies. I didn't have the same shape as before having children and was very insecure. I saw myself as an ugly woman. So I decided to do something about it. I decided to have breast augmentation.

Several months later, I woke up in the recovery room feeling like a beautiful, new woman. A "New Me!" I did it. My breast augmentation surgery was a success. My confidence soared as I held my head high, pleased with the results.

But approximately two years into my newfound body, things began to change.

I first noticed I was getting sick often, which was unusual as I had always been a very healthy and fit woman. And then I began to gain weight. I was big into lifting weights and trained hard to have the perfect body, but exercising now didn't help me lose the pounds.

To my dismay, I knew something was wrong with me. Over the next thirteen years, my health declined. I began to have muscle and joint pain, chronic fatigue, memory and concentration problems, sleep disturbance, rashes, skin problems, dry eyes, anxiety, depression, headaches, hair loss, weight gain, gastrointestinal issues, and enlarged lymph nodes. The symptoms continued to increase the older I became.

Finally, in 2014, I had an adrenal crash that took me to the hospital emergency room. I was diagnosed as dehydrated. How could this be? I drank three to four liters of water daily. I figured the diagnosis must be incorrect.

When I followed up with my doctor, I presented him with three pages full of issues I'd experienced for years.

"What do you want me to do?" He asked flippantly, then added, "There's nothing wrong with you."

Time and time again, I heard these exact words as I looked for answers from the experts.

I believe doctors are a blessing and can help us. However, I knew I would have to go a different route to find answers. So, I sought a naturopathic doctor, who confirmed that my adrenals were shot. She was educated to help others restore their adrenal function properly and directed me to eat certain foods and take supplements to return my adrenals to good health. Natural healing was the right choice for me, and although this seemed to help, I still continued having many of the same issues. Not feeling well became my normal state. I learned to live with it.

Life continued, and one Thursday morning in early 2021, during a women's Bible study, a lady talked about her recent "explant"—a medical procedure performed by a board-certified plastic surgeon to remove breast implants. She shared how she felt so much better and how her pre-surgery symptoms were going away.

I began to wonder: *Could my implants be causing my issues? Should I have them taken out?* The thought of getting them removed was scary. *What would I look like?* I wasn't ready to acknowledge that this may be the answer to my thirteen-year health battle. Hence, I put the thought aside.

Then, a year later, I was under some stress, and my adrenals became an issue again. Severe rashes, like second-degree burns, appeared on my arms. I was getting sick and having frequent ear and respiratory infections. Towards the end of 2022, my body was shutting down. I couldn't remember simple things. Brain fog overtook my mind. I wasn't able to read a book or my Bible. I struggled to comprehend the simplest tasks. I had severe back and neck pain and developed scoliosis in my spine. My left upper arm was in constant pain, and I was losing sleep.

In December 2022, I experienced symptoms of Transient Ischemic Attach (TIA)—mini-strokes. I went to the emergency room, only to be told again there was nothing wrong with me and that I should see my doctor and have my thyroid medication adjusted. I felt like I was back to square one. The doctors didn't have the answers I needed. I was very frustrated. I knew sickness wasn't from the Lord because Jesus took the stripes for our healing. I believed His Word is true. I believed all Jesus did for me at the cross. So why was I not getting healed? I didn't have the answers. However, I trusted I would be healed at some point.

Shortly after my ER visit, I attended a Bible college class. While I praised the Lord during worship, my back and neck throbbed with excruciating pain. I couldn't stand it any longer. I sat back in my chair and closed my eyes. All I could pray was, "Lord, help."

Suddenly, with an urgency in my spirit, I heard, "Get them out. Get them out!"

I understood. *Get the implants out!*

Later, a friend's Facebook post about Breast Implant Illness (BII) confirmed my suspicion. I researched BII, and what I found blew my mind!

Everything I had been going through for the last thirteen years was on the BII signs and symptoms list, including hypothyroidism and autoimmune disease, which I had been diagnosed with.

I was finally beginning to get answers. *Thank you, Jesus!* Day in and day out, I read every website on BII. I joined several Facebook groups to hear others' stories, including those who had symptoms similar to mine. The stories I read assured me I wasn't a hypochondriac. However, finding answers became an obsession and affected me in many ways. Most notably, I took my eyes off Jesus.

I immediately found a surgeon in West Palm Beach, Florida, and scheduled my surgery for February 21, 2023. I had total peace.

But just days later, negative thoughts again attacked my mind. This time, they were different from my regular cutdowns about myself.

> *And do not be conformed to this world, but be transformed by the renewing of your mind, that you may prove what is that good and acceptable and perfect will of God* (Romans 12:2 NKJV).

This time, I heard, "You're going to die! You won't wake up from surgery!"

Nightmares of seeing myself buried in a grave paralyzed me with fear. I was afraid to go to sleep, so I left a light on at night. I felt like I was spinning as if on an airplane falling from the sky, unable to determine my direction, whether facing up or down. My tailspin was such an example of how the enemy can work. It started slow, and the next thing, I was falling and didn't know what hit me. I didn't want to tell anyone. I didn't want to be judged. As a Christian, I knew better than to believe the lies. I just needed to take authority over the devil. Right? The horrific dreams and infiltrating thoughts persisted nightly, and I continued to hold onto the hem of Jesus' cloak.

I cried for help from the Lord, and He heard me.

The night before my explant, I chanted in my sleep, "I believe You, God—because You'll finish what You started. I will trust You."

I awoke the morning of the surgery knowing God was with me. When the Holy Spirit tells us to do something, we can be assured He will be with us. He will not allow anything to happen to us. He has already made a way. All we have to do is be obedient to His instructions. The overwhelming peace I felt while praising the Lord on the way to the surgery center brought me to tears. I found hope in the middle of my chaos!

"For I will restore health to you, and your wounds I will heal, declares the Lord, because they have called you an outcast: 'It is Zion, for whom no one cares!'" (Jeremiah 30:17 ESV).

The explant procedure took four and a half hours. When I woke up, I could breathe! I was alive!

My health improved tremendously in such a short period. Before surgery, I was pale. Two days after, my color came back. The whites of my eyes were restored to their original color. My hair stopped falling out and continues to grow back. My comprehension and memory are returning. I'm rereading my Bible and seeing His Word with fresh revelations. Each day something new is restored. Praise the Lord!

I am in awe of what God has done and continues to do in my healing process.

Ten years ago, I started my journey to know who Jesus is. He has revealed His goodness, love, and mercy and has shown me that His grace is sufficient for me. I knew He would never leave me because He was always there when I felt so alone. Even when I saw myself as ugly, fat, and unable to do anything right, He saw me as His beautiful creation. He called me His beloved friend. He made a way when I didn't think there was a way. When I hurt, He hurt.

Today, I rejoice in the Lord, for I am His beloved. I am His daughter, and He is my everything.

I am no longer who I thought I was. I am who He says I am!

I am Kimberly, daughter of the Most High. I am a King! I have been made in the image of God. He calls me by my name. I am beautiful, successful, creative, and talented in His eyes. I can do all things through Christ Jesus, who gives me strength—all power and authority have been given to me to overcome the devil. I have the mind of Christ, and the Holy Spirit dwells within me. Most of all, I am His, and He loves me.

The following is something the Lord placed in my heart; it isn't just for me. Receive a fresh word from the Lord, my friend.

> *You are my beloved, and I will walk with you through the process of your healing, Stay in my presence and let me do the rest.*
>
> *I love you, my daughter. I am in you, and you are in Me.*
>
> *Be still and know that I am your God, who is with you day and night.*

I will never leave you or forsake you. Trust in Me always.

You are not the past. You are the present; this is you now. Look how far you have come.

You are a new creation in Christ Jesus, all things are new, and the old has passed away and is gone. It is dead!

When I died, You died with Me. When I rose from the dead, you rose with Me. When I sat down at the right hand of the Father, you sat there, too.

Continue to grow, My beloved. Continue to grow.

My beloved, join Me in this celebration—knowing you are free! You are free indeed!

Come to Me, all who are thirsty, for your Father in heaven is waiting for you. I love you!

Finding the Miracle in Loss

by Julie T. Jenkins

Loss is a part of life. But it is one of those agonizing things we wish we didn't have to endure. Suffering the loss of a job, a pet, a relationship, a season of life, or even a loved one can lead to unwelcome grief and sadness.

If you are going through a time of grief, it would be wrong of me to throw a cliché at you such as, "You are probably better off," "Better to have loved and lost," or even, "She's in a better place." Our feelings are real. And they are valid. And sometimes, we all just need to cry.

But although loss is real—and often really painful—when we walk through our grief with a Miracle Mindset, God will bring good from our grief, purpose from our pain, and life even amid our loss.

GOOD FROM OUR GRIEF

What possible good can come from our grief? Here's the brutal truth: God cares more about your relationship with Him than your daily comfort. That can be a tough pill to swallow in today's egocentric society. We all think we know what we want: we want the easy life, the luxuries, and the lack of pain. But God wants so much more for you.

Psalm 34:18 states, *The Lord is close to the brokenhearted and saves those who are crushed in spirit* (NIV).

This is a fascinating statement to unpack. As followers of Jesus Christ, we hold the belief that God is close to us all the time, not just when we are brokenhearted. So why is this stated this way?

Perhaps it is because we often get so caught up in life that we drift away from the close relationship God wants to have with us.

The Message states Psalm 34:18 this way: *If your heart is broken, you'll find God right there; if you're kicked in the gut, he'll help you catch your breath.*

Now that is something we can hold onto in our grief! It's as if God moves us into a Miracle Mindset, teaching us that when everything else fails, He never will. As we walk through our grief, God will infuse our souls with the truth that He is with us at every step and that He alone can provide everything we need. Being granted the reminder of God's ever-presence in our lives is a miraculous good God wants to bring out of our grief.

PURPOSE FROM OUR PAIN

Have you ever experienced a loss so profound that you were left stunned by the depth of your pain? Loss can open a chasm within us that cries out to be filled.

As excruciating as it is, this chasm gives us the opportunity to reevaluate where God is calling us and what He wants us to do in the next season. As we cry out to God for direction, He will awaken a miracle of purpose within us. This book is filled with stories of an empty chasm created by pain that led to a new beginning—one that God used to help someone else, even pointing them to the healing balm of Jesus Christ.

> *I consider that our present sufferings are not worth comparing with the glory that will be revealed in us* (Romans 8:18 NIV).

LIFE AMID OUR LOSS

As contrary as it sounds, God can use our loss to give life!

Recently, my mom died after a long battle with Alzheimer's. For over ten years, I grieved as memories evaporated from her mind. I often cried out to God, not understanding the purpose of this type of illness. But when she did die, I felt her full life return! I knew, beyond a shadow of a doubt, that God had finally made her whole. I can now feel her presence with me—complete, as she once was. Dying returned her to life.

Often the transition to life-giving loss is not so readily apparent. Perhaps that is because we cannot fathom, with our human brains, how amazing God's life-giving spirit is. The truth is, God only wants the best for us, and when we lose something, painful though it might be, we can trust that He is holding us and will offer us life beyond our darkest nights.

By developing a Miracle Mindset—intentionally looking for the miracles all around us—God will begin to illuminate the fullness of the life He has ahead of us. When one door closes, we can trust that our sovereign God will open the next right door. And when your path is blocked, it is because God has a different one destined just for you.

Loss is difficult—there is no doubt about it. But as Christians, we can hold to the fact that God always has miracles waiting to carry us to a new beginning. When you find yourself in a season of loss, nestle close to Jesus. Weep and mourn as long as you need to, but do so with an open mind, receptive to His healing and care. And if you let Him, in time, Jesus will bring good from your grief, purpose from your pain, and life even amid your loss.

. . . .

THAYSE EDGETT PRICE

Thayse Edgett Price is a wife, daughter, sister, and friend who loves unconditionally and is passionate about sharing the gospel of Jesus Christ. She attended Bethel College in Redding, California, and was a missionary before becoming a waitress.

Thayse enjoys meeting new people and learning about new cultures. Her life has been an incredible journey so far, full of growth, adventure, and experiences that have shaped her into the person she is today.

Thayse is currently getting involved in her local church, waiting for what God has for her and her family in this next season of ministry. She is passionate about creating healthy families and creating community.

TRUST THE PROCESS

by Thayse Edgett Price

Every little girl dreams of being a princess—a beautiful, elegant princess worthy of being whisked away by her very own Prince Charming. But as we grow older, often our self-esteem gets beaten down, and the girl who once envisioned herself as royalty may focus on her flaws and begin to see herself as inferior.

Society distorts our view of ourselves. It also taints our morals and what we deem to be important. For example, television, social media, and marketing tell us that promiscuity and nudity are acceptable. And sometimes, the church—the other extreme—gives women an unrealistic view of how a perfect spouse is supposed to look. These polar opposite ideologies can be troubling, and as I grew up, they left me feeling confused, full of self-doubt, and void of self-worth.

Some girls grow up without a father to instill self-worth in them. Likewise, some grow up without mothers who are secure in themselves and, consequently, able to help their daughters develop a healthy mindset of who they are in Christ. Unfortunately, my childhood did not include either a mom or dad to teach me the values and morals of Jesus Christ.

I did not have a healthy example of a family. My biological mother had no clue how to mother, raise a family, or create a safe home filled with love. She married several times, and I never really knew her well. As a result, I was afraid to pursue a family of my own, having no idea what a healthy family looked like. My biggest fear? Turning out like my mother. I didn't want to make the same mistakes she did, so I became fearful of being in a committed relationship.

But God was always there for me. Because that is who He is.

I finally met and fell in love with Jesus in my late teens when God graciously and miraculously brought me into my spiritual family, who cared for me as their own. They adopted me into their forever family and helped reshape my mindset about who I am in Christ.

Although we got a late start together, my mom taught me how to be a respectful and thoughtful woman. She taught me how to cook and bake. She taught me how to behave in public—as funny as that might sound, that was something I didn't know how to do before she poured into me.

On the other hand, my dad taught me how to be strong. He taught me to make better decisions and have higher expectations for the men I would date. As I grew into adulthood, nurtured by their love, I began to yearn for a family of my own—something I had feared for so long.

I watched the way my spiritual parents behaved. After four decades of marriage, they are still so in love with each other. There isn't one thing they wouldn't do for one another. I wanted a marriage like theirs, one where my husband would love me unconditionally for who I am and be someone I could love the same way. Deep inside, I wanted a partner who would see me and love me for who God created me to be. He would empower the calling over my life.

As a child, true love had been a foreign concept to me. But when I said Yes to Jesus in my late teens, I began to experience God's love and understand the depth of love that is possible for each of us. I read my Bible and longed to model my life after the woman who poured the costly perfume on the feet of Jesus. I aspired to be a woman with a heart after Jesus, one who gives and loves the only way she knows how—with everything!

> *Then Mary took about a pint of pure nard, an expensive perfume; she poured it on Jesus' feet and wiped his feet with her hair. And the house was filled with the fragrance of the perfume* (John 12:3 NIV).

As I grew in my relationship with the Lord, I felt called to be a missionary. God told me I would change nations for Him, and I set out to obey Him. I poured myself out at the feet of Jesus. In those years, I learned to love myself. And I learned to depend on God for every little thing. Signs, wonders, and miracles occurred in almost every country I served. God used me in amazing ways, and I will never be the same. I was an unequipped girl from the Amazon jungle who had grown into accepting and abiding by His love. What my spiritual, adopted parents imparted to me, I was able to impart to the nations.

Each time I left for a new location to share God's name, I felt so happy and joyous. And I would return so spiritually fulfilled. As I grew in Christ, my longing for a family of my own continued to grow stronger. At times I'd sit with my dad and cry, wondering why no man wanted anything to do with me. Prophetic words spoken over me proffered a healthy family in my future, but I had no man, no marriage, and no children. When I cried at the feet of my dad, he told me, "Thayse, you are beautiful. One day a man will see the treasure within you. You will make an amazing wife."

When I returned from my last mission trip, I sensed things in my life were about to change. My friend had just opened a restaurant and invited me to work for them. After I began my new job, I met an amazing man. He stole my heart right away. He was so kind and had such a big personality. We immediately became friends and soon started to date.

We experienced all of my favorite things together. We attended church together. We studied the Bible together. He evangelized with me. Little by little, I recognized in him all of the things I had wanted in a man. My family liked him, and he loved all the same things my dad loved. We became so close and inseparable; the direction my life was going became clear. God aligned our lives and our hearts. This man loved me so well and treated me with utter respect.

After eight months of dating and planning our future together, an accident shattered my whole world. My parents and I drove to the hospital to hear the news: my fiancé—the love of my life—was with the Lord. My heart was so broken. My family was sad. I became so angry at God. I was sure that if I just prayed hard enough, God would resurrect him, like He did Lazarus. But the man I had waited for my whole life was gone. I couldn't comprehend it. I was devastated. I went from being in a state of uncaring faith to a place of complete anger. How dare God give me such a great gift and then take it away.

I spent weeks and months on the couch, not knowing what direction to go. Once again, despite having many people around me, I felt so lonely. I felt robbed of a great future. But I reasoned that everything happens for a reason and finally came to grips that now he was in heaven. My heart still hurts when I think of it. For an entire year, I wasn't able to sleep or eat very much. I hoped the pain would go away, but it did not. I don't think it will ever go away completely. I battled thoughts of suicide and so much anxiety.

I went from being an *on-fire* missionary to someone who questioned God. The process was so painful.

During that time, I started to journal. I logged every thought in the journal I kept beside my bed. I wrote God very angry letters. I was losing myself, and I knew I needed help. I needed to heal my heart, but I didn't know how. I reached out to someone who was able to help me emotionally and spiritually. I had a long history with Papa God, and I was determined that no one or nothing would steal that from me.

Slowly God began to shift my mindset. I recorded declarations on my phone and listened to them daily, sometimes multiple times a day. I wrote out God's promises and taped them to my car, to my phone, and anywhere that would remind me of His goodness. Whenever I cried out to my dad, he reminded me of God's faithfulness. God was not done with me yet. My mom was so kind and patient in this process. My brothers always encouraged me. God knew exactly who I needed in my life.

As time passed, things started to feel a little more normal; slowly, my hope began to grow. I spent a lot of time in prayer, asking God to change my heart and make me stronger. My brothers and dad were such beautiful representations of what faithful Christian men should look like. The Bible says that a man is to care for his family, love his wife, and train his kids in the way they should go. I'm grateful God planted me in this family so I could witness this firsthand.

Over the course of a decade or so, I wrote a book of prayers and declarations God gave me for my future husband. I believed God was speaking to me about him through my prayers about his life. I dreamed of one day giving him the writings that flowed from the depths of my soul. But over time, it seemed I'd never have another opportunity to open my heart again, so I put the book aside. I wanted nothing to do with it.

But the Lord wasn't done healing my heart, and a few months later, He led me to take a different approach to life. I started trying to find myself again, doing things I hadn't yet done. Life was too short, and I was too young to let life pass me by. I started going on trips for fun, not just for ministry. I started a health journey—getting up early to run and work out. I called friends I hadn't talked to in many years. I even began to speak words of encouragement into other people's lives. As I did, I met women in the same situation as myself. I chose to trust God in the process.

It's crazy how life happens so quickly. Every day I had to make an active choice to continue trusting God even though I was still so very angry at Him. I was blessed to have incredible people in my life to challenge me and push me forward to the fullness of my potential. My desire was still set on having a family of my own, a dream that had been stolen from me but would later be remedied by God. I learned that God had given me the will and desire to always fight for family.

We live in a world where there are many different standards of family morality. In this time of confusion, God's standards of moral cleanliness are often misconstrued by society. Yet nothing changes with God, for He is the same yesterday, today, and forever. Recognizing this, I came to the conclusion that I was called to work to preserve the family as God designed it.

I also began to recognize that central to keeping our families intact is keeping our bodies sacred. The Lord has given us bodies for a divine purpose. He expects us to keep them clean and worthy to receive His Spirit. It is our job to teach the protection of purity, treating those we befriend and choose to date like kings and queens. It wasn't until my late teens that I had learned the importance of keeping myself pure for my future spouse, which wasn't always an easy task but has been rewarding. And as my own childhood exemplifies, today's world threatens to break up the family foundation. But

God has called and equipped us to protect the family unit. I began to recognize that despite my past, God anointed me to create a healthy family. That is something I'm willing to fight for it. My spiritual, adopted parents' marriage is my example. As a member of the family, I have had a front-row seat to watch my parents' marriage. I hoped to put into practice what I learned from them.

Holding to these beliefs and values God instilled in me, I strived to live with a victorious mindset. One thing I worked on was intentionally changing my word choices; this helped shift my old patterns and behaviors, which, over time, had created a negative mindset. By adjusting my words and behavior—including the way I treated others—Jesus was able to shine through me.

After a year of getting to know myself again—by taking myself out on dates and working through the grief—hope came alive within me once more. Over the holiday season, I watched the television series When Calls the Heart, and I could sense my heart changing. I began again to desire to be a homemaker. I wanted to experience being in love and being pursued.

I made the decision to join a social app with the hopes of making new friends. I just wanted a friend or two with whom I could do fun things. Soon after this step, I was ready to explore dating again. The app matched me up with a young man. We talked for a few weeks on the phone, and later that month, I agreed to go on a date. I played it super safe—I had parents on standby and shared my location with every family member. Just in case. We talked forever and had such a nice time. I left that evening wondering, Is this it? Have I found my Prince Charming?

I went home and prayed. I told Jesus, *If this is the man You have for me, You have to make him who You have promised me, the promise of what my husband would be like.*

The night after meeting him, I wrote in my journal that if this man was not willing to walk into what God created him to be, then I wanted no part of the relationship. If he wasn't prepared to respect me and my spirituality and who God created me to be, I didn't want him. And I made that very clear to him.

On our first date, we talked about all the *do's* and *don'ts*. Politics. Religion. Money. Kids. All of it! Our future was laid out before our eyes that first evening. I guess it's true that when you meet the one person you're going to spend your whole life with, things just click.

On our third date, I invited him to tag along with me to visit a friend in Colorado. To my surprise, he said, "Yes." We spent three days having the time of our lives and getting to know each other better—with separate room arrangements, of course. After that, we became inseparable. We did everything together. He started attending my church and doing all of the things I love to do. At first, I thought he just wanted to impress me, but it turned out he was looking for something greater than himself. God orchestrated that first date that changed our lives forever.

Last summer, we got engaged. Three months later, my dad walked me down the aisle. My dad—the one who taught me how a man should treat his family. The man who loved me through my ups and downs. The man who gave me value as a daughter. *The dad I never had* walked me down the aisle in tears. I was so grateful! My biggest prayer had become my reality. I just needed to trust the process.

This is not the end, but I know beyond a shadow of a doubt that God has brought me here to my greatest calling. He took my life and turned ashes into beauty, valuing me as HIS princess, worthy by His call to be whisked away into His love for eternity. Our God is a miracle-working God who provides His children with more than we can ask or imagine. We can each live every day as royalty, walking through the ups and downs with a miracle mindset as we seek and trust our King of kings.

Finding the Miracle in Loneliness

by Julie T. Jenkins

"We were made for community."

You have likely heard that message taught as the Bible states this implicitly and explicitly throughout its pages.

In the beginning, God made Eve to be Adam's helper. *The Lord God said, "It is not good for the man to be alone. I will make a helper suitable for him"* (Genesis 2:18 NIV).

God promised Abraham that he would be the father of many, saying, *"I will make you into a great nation, and I will bless you"* (Genesis 12:2 NIV).

Jesus chose twelve disciples to accompany Him during His time on earth and, when He died, made sure that His mother, Mary, and His disciple, John, would care for each other (John 19:26-27).

So if we are "made for community," is it possible to find a miracle in loneliness?

Loneliness indicates a sadness that overcomes us when we are alone. Being alone and being lonely are two very different things. Some people relish being alone. Introverts gain energy from being by themselves. For some, being alone can be exhilarating and is even preferred to being with others.

But for others, and likely for us all at times, being alone can lead to loneliness and even feelings of depression or unworthiness. This reality became so apparent during the worldwide COVID-19 lockdown. Still, feeling lonely is certainly not new, and it is an ongoing issue as people continue to be isolated due to age, mobile ability, loss of close relationships, or even fears or finances. It isn't even necessary to be physically alone to experience loneliness; we can also be emotionally lonely—simply *feeling* alone.

Whatever the cause of loneliness, we should never dismiss or make light of our emotions. If you are feeling depressed or stricken with other unbearable symptoms, reach out to your church (or any Bible-believing church), a counselor or therapist, or a family member or neighbor. We were not meant to do life alone, and you can know for certain that God has someone waiting in the wings of your life, ready to meet you where you are. Pray to God; He will guide you in the right direction for the connections He has waiting for you.

But even as you ask God to step in and heal your loneliness, if you set your mind on seeing His miracles, you may recognize something that has never occurred to you.

Jesus, our Lord and Savior, wants to be your best friend! He is always with you, loves you more than you can imagine, knows exactly what you need when you need it, and will provide, protect, and defend you whenever you turn to Him.

What if, as we turn to Jesus asking Him to kick our loneliness to the curb, we begin to understand the miracle that we have never been alone? God is our ever-present companion!

God the Father is always with you to love and protect you. The Holy Spirit dwells within you, leading and guiding you. And Jesus, who lived on this earth as a human being, understands your feelings and emotions firsthand and is always available to offer you salvation, grace, mercy, peace, and joy as you walk through each moment of your life.

> *The Lord your God goes with you; he will never leave you nor forsake you* (Deuteronomy 31:6 NIV).

Being lonely is painful, but the blessed Holy Trinity—Father, Son, and Holy Spirit—can use this emotion to remind us that we are NEVER alone. God is always with us.

As you read this book, our prayer is that you will become more and more miracle minded—that you will look for and see God and all His miracles in both good and bad times. But perhaps the simple miracle of God's presence is most apparent when we experience loneliness. Just as a jeweler places a diamond on a black velvet cloth to illuminate the gem's brilliance, so the light of God's presence beckons us to Him when our world seems darkest.

As you cry out to God in your loneliness, seeking community, pry your thoughts from the darkness and look for the miracle of His brilliant light.

God is there.

You are not alone.

. . . .

KEILY J. DENNY

Keily J. Denny was born and raised in Boston, Massachusetts, and now resides in Murfreesboro, Tennessee, with her husband of 34 years. She is the founder and CEO of Stroke Community Alliance, a 501c3 organization that partners with companies, individuals, and agencies to provide resources, goods, services, and financial assistance to stroke victims and their families. (www.strokecommunityalliance.org, info@strokecommunityalliance.org)

Keily is an avid writer who contributes devotions to Women World Leaders. She enjoys serving the Lord by encouraging others to find their God-given purpose and is a gifted prophetic intercessor and healing evangelist. Also known by her stage name Snugumspooh, Keily performs as a stand-up comedian and spoken word artist. She's featured regularly on *The Lit Comedy Club,* hosted on the social media platform Clubhouse.

Having recently added a home studio, Keily is launching her new podcast and venturing into voiceover work and other creative projects. She is truly grateful God allows her to use ALL her gifts to send hope and healing into the world and bring others closer to Him!

Follow Keily J. Denny, aka Snugumspooh, on Instagram, Facebook, Twitter, TikTok, YouTube, and Clubhouse. She's available to perform at your next event, contact her at keily@keilyjdenny.com, and stay up-to-date with her at www.keilyjdenny.com

DIVINE PROVIDENCE

by Keily J. Denny

For our struggle is not against flesh and blood, but against the rulers, against the authorities, against the powers of this dark world and against the spiritual forces of evil in the heavenly realms (Ephesians 6:12 NIV).

There is a bitter war on earth between the demonic realm and the kingdom of God, and we are all called to stand against the forces of evil. This can be more difficult than we can imagine, but God will always be with us, ready to work miracles on our behalf.

The Lord has endowed me with the gift of sight. So, when I received a scholarship to go to a well-known Healing Evangelist's school in September 2016, I jumped at the chance. Then, when I returned home in mid-January 2017, I was exhausted. After living in Fort Mill, South Carolina four long months, I was looking forward to resting my body, mind, and soul. I needed to unwind and reflect. But, as soon as I stepped foot into my house, I saw that it looked like a rehab project from a house flipper's show.

While I was away, our water filtration system caused a flood inside 95% of our house. All of the carpets, the bottoms of the walls, and bedroom furniture needed to be replaced. This was a disaster—simply not something my husband and I could handle on our own. Thankfully, we didn't have to—the Lord gave us a strategy and was with us at every step.

I am not a stranger to dealing with the demonic realm or angels from heaven. Both are real, and I've had my encounters with them. So, my husband and I walked through our house and performed spiritual house cleaning. Once we were done worshipping, decreeing various scriptures, and taking authority over the neighborhood, we smelled a very strong odor of burning firewood throughout the house—each room felt noticeably warmer. At one point, I felt like I was about to pass out from the heat.

God then sent a messenger who told me to get my house in order. I thought that meant deep cleaning and decluttering the house. But I was not prepared for the wild rollercoaster ride the Lord was about to take us on for the next seven years.

Holy Spirit had been prompting us to sell the house and move. To say that my husband was reluctant about that would be an understatement. Furthermore, we did not have the finances to do all of the indoor and outdoor repairs that were now necessary to prepare the house for sale.

To make matters worse, both our cars were on their last legs—you could hear me coming a mile away! But the Lord gave me the strategy to refinance the house and pull out a little equity. We pulled out just enough to buy two much younger used cars and do some house repairs. We did all of this, yet our mortgage payment remained the same because the interest rates had gone way down from what we were originally paying. Praise God that He is always in control, and when we walk righteously with Him, He gives us His power to deal with anything that is thrown at us.

The prayer of a righteous person is powerful and effective (James 5:16 NIV).

All believers, come here and listen, let me tell you what God did for me. I called out to him with my mouth, my tongue shaped the sounds of music. If I had been cozy with evil, the Lord would never have listened. But he most surely did listen, he came on the double when he heard my prayer. Blessed be God: he didn't turn a deaf ear, he stayed with me, loyal in his love (Psalm 66:16-20 MSG).

Next, we aggressively repaired EVERYTHING that could hinder the sale. As we did, the trouble kept coming, but God's power remained, overcoming each obstacle as quickly as it appeared, often before we were aware of an impending issue!

As the contractor tore down rotten wood in our fascia, he saw two hornet's nests. One was the size of an adult human brain, and the other was the size of a grapefruit. When he knocked them down, a bunch of hornets chased him around the yard, and many flew back up inside the house. We had no idea that there were that many hornets in our attic. If we had gone up there, we would have been trapped and gotten stung multiple times. Likely, the hornets would have infiltrated our entire house through the drop-down entry into the attic from the hallway. Things could have gotten extremely dangerous for us. The pest control guy told us hornets are very aggressive, and we could've accidentally bumped into their nest or something. But, God!

Then, the air conditioning technician who replaced our old unit discovered we had a gas leak that had likely been there for years. None of the previous HVAC techs had ever mentioned this, despite us having had bi-annual maintenance done regularly. We could have died from this leak. And in retrospect, we believe we were showing the effects of gas poisoning (brain fog, smelling gas fumes at times), but God protected us.

Once the two enormous nests got removed and the gas leak was resolved, I noticed a tremendous difference in my emotions—I became calmer and felt more at ease. I think I felt an alarm going off in my spirit because of the danger we were in.

Then, due to a pipe burst on the main water valve, there were 1-2 feet of water in our 1780 sq foot crawl space. It looked like we would need to spend a few thousand dollars to get it pumped—a 3-day job that would encompass mold removal and drying out fees. BUT I SERVE A GOD WHO ANSWERS THE PRAYERS OF THE RIGHTEOUS! We said, "The devil is a liar! Oh no, it's not, in Jesus' name!"

As soon as the plumber turned off the water, the flood in our crawlspace started receding. Within the two hours it took him to install the new pipe, the water was almost completely gone—miraculously draining into the ground! Only a few small puddles remained. The plumber told us it would dry out with no mold worries! This only cost us $75, and our water was quickly restored!

> *"They will fight against you but will not overcome you, for I am with you and will rescue you," declares the Lord* (Jeremiah 1:19 NIV).

Satan was not giving up.

- In the midst of preparing the house for sale, my husband of over 25 years and I began to grow very distant. We were fussing and fighting quite a bit; it turned ugly. We were headed for divorce court.

- While I was packing up the house at a feverish pace, I hurt my back. When I went to a chiropractor, they overdid a spinal traction and made things worse, so I was in excruciating pain.

- My only child began to verbally attack me and withhold my grandchildren from me.

- My mother's kidneys were failing to function, so she was placed in a nursing home 1,000 miles away from where I lived—in another state.

- I began to have anxiety attacks, fainting spells, and narcoleptic fits. On top of that, I had bouts of deep depression.

- My husband was a blue-collar worker with mandatory overtime, causing him to work seven days a week for months in a row with no days off. The arthritis in both his hips was exacerbated by all the required standing during that mandatory overtime, resulting in him needing two hip replacements, one month apart from each other. I had to take care of him while I was dealing with all of these issues.

I think the devil was mad. What do you think?

Then, the unthinkable happened: COVID-19 hit, and the world changed as we knew it! People started dying as fear gripped the whole world! My husband and I had to stick it out—we were forced to stay together and learn how to communicate and get along.

When I think on these things, it occurs to me that I have been praying for many years for everything hidden in the dark to be brought to the light and commanding all demons to come out of their hiding places in my home or my life and get out, in the name of Jesus! How many times do we pray without REALLY, TRULY understanding the power of prayer and the authority that Jesus died on the cross to give us? Be careful what you pray for!

All of these things were breaches that were being exposed. This is what God meant when He sent me the message to get my house in order. It had a duality—I was to clean both my dwelling place and my temple.

It took us five years to complete all the repairs, throw things away, and pack. We finally sold the house in December 2021.

God's timing is perfect. The housing market had shot through the roof in our area, and we were able to totally get out of debt, buy another house, buy all new furniture and appliances, and have a studio in the backyard with enough money left over to start a new business and take classes to run it.

We both caught COVID-19 while we were scheduled to close on our home. My husband had a very mild case, but I was hospitalized for a week and could've died from COVID pneumonia and blood clots. Although I felt winded, very weak, and riddled with residual symptoms such as labored breathing, brain fog, and fatigue, our progress was not hampered. Not only was I able to go house hunting two days after I got out of the hospital, but while we lived in a hotel for four months, I was able to drive around looking for houses, make calls, and think straight about anything that had to do with finding us a new home. However, as soon as I stopped that activity, I returned to feeling residual brain fog and fatigue. I continuously saw firsthand what the Lord meant when He proclaimed to the apostle Paul that when we are weak, He is strong! (2 Corinthians 12:10 NIV). Thank you for being strong FOR me, my Jesus! How I love you!

We finally found a house that we fell in love with. We made a strong offer! The morning the bidding was to close, Holy Spirit told me to increase our bid by $5,000 and add a clause stating that the seller could remain in the home for 30 days at no charge. There were 11 bids on the house. We beat out the highest bidder, who had offered $5,000 more than we had because we included the extra 30 days. The seller needed the additional time more than they needed the extra $5,000. We received the news that we won the bid for the house in the evening on Valentine's Day, February 14, 2022. Holy Spirit's melodramatic display of love for us was precisely what we needed!

The battle wasn't yet over. We ended up offering $25,000 above the asking price, and the neighborhood comps were much lower. We needed the house appraisal to match our offer or our loan would only cover the original asking price and we would have to come up with an additional $25,000 cash above all of the fees and closing costs. So we fasted and prayed and asked all of our praying friends to intercede.

Two weeks later, the entire neighborhood's value skyrocketed; the house appraised for exactly what we offered. The banker and realtor were amazed; they said they had never seen that happen in the history of the business! $100,000 out of pocket at closing plummeted to $79,000! My Daddy changed the financial forecast of the neighborhood just before our appraisal date!! Saints, He'll make a way when there seems to be no way! Do what He says and pray to trust Him in a way that brings peace of mind even though things look less than favorable for you! He had told us where to move, and we did! Obedience brings provision!

The last hurdle was for the house to pass the various inspections. The night before, my husband and I prayed, "Lord, let us feel like it was a waste of time and money when we hear the reports from each type of inspection." Beloved, there was absolutely nothing wrong with this house that $150 could not fix!

Next, I needed to turn the shed into a recording/tv studio. I was running into bids from $10,000 to $25,000. A friend I had met years before at a Christian Film Breakfast Club heard about my plight and offered to do what I needed for $2500. He had experience building studios in Hollywood and had a few tricks up his sleeve. Because of my obedience to go to that meeting several years ago, he was already in position to help me in this extreme time of need!

The Lord's divine providence is CLEARLY in control of my life! As you can see, there were so many ways that God provided for us, and, believe it or not, I haven't shared them all! Stay tuned for a book about the wonders of God's miracles in my life in the near future!

I went through a season of spiritual deconstruction (brokenness) and reconstruction (surgery and healing). Everything that could be shaken was shaken—my faith, my marriage, my health, my family relationships— EVERY area in my life! One of the most treasured outcomes from all this was that God gave me a renewed love for my husband! Even when we fell out of love, he was still a good friend and was always there for me!

This new phase is going to be the phase of giving birth to multiples for me. Every breach will be revealed, healed, and sealed! Revival is eminent for me and my house, in Jesus' name!

Beloved, I have spent decades toiling, tilling, weeding, watering, sowing, fertilizing, travailing, healing, growing, learning, and being pruned; going through flames of purification and several furnaces of affliction. Whew! I am so happy to report the reaping has come! It's REAPING TIME!!!

The fact that I am a contributing author in this book you are reading right now solidifies the fact that I am what He says I am.

Many years ago, God had called to me, proclaiming me a writer. And true to His word, it has now come to pass! He did so many things to assure that I arrived at this place—that is why He guided our steps to be in THIS house! He provided me with a studio so that I can have a place to give birth to all of the creative babies that His Spirit has impregnated me with! Podcasts, skits, videos, short films, voiceover and spoken word projects, comedic skits, interviews—the sky is the limit! I am both humbled and thunderstruck at how much He trusts me with these delicate matters. I do not take it lightly!

The song of my soul is to help someone in need. The melody is the sound of their sigh of relief. The lyrics are the words of encouragement. The rhythm is the sound of resuscitation of their hope with a heart beating with the blood of Jesus! For such a time as this, my acts of obedience roar beyond obstacles and hindrances and reverberate the frequency of breakthrough! The juicy fruit of Salvation is served and, for the recipient, it tastes so sweet! Thank you for this honor, my Lord, my King!

Birthing this baby has set the tone for what is to come! It is my time! It is my turn! No imp in hell can stop it! Heaven is with me! With God on my side, who and what can be against me?

May it be unto you as it is for me, in Jesus' name! May fresh fire fall and burn up everything that holds you bound!

The timer is set, the sand dial is emptying, and destiny is on the other side of midnight! A new dispensation of time, grace, and strength is set into motion. Get ready; clothe yourself in strength! Wash your soul with hope; water your faith with the positivity of Jesus, The Word. It has begun! Come, Holy Spirit.

Blow the shofar, sound the trumpets, release a sound of VICTORY!! For the King of Glory, Jehovah Gibbor, The Lord of Armies, is on the scene! Alleluia!

Finding the Miracle in Financial Hardship

by Kelley Rene

Many of us have experienced it. Likely more than once. A time when money was tight or nonexistent. A miracle in your finances may have seemed as unlikely as winning the lottery. But you could always hope, right?

In the early days of my marriage, I budgeted our income in a single-lined ledger notebook. We juggled car payments, college loans, and all the incidentals of adulting. We committed to putting extra income toward our debts in order to pay them off as quickly as possible. We didn't dine out, buy new clothes, or go to the movies. We were intentional about watching our dollars and going to God with our financial needs.

This strategy was not a foreign concept to me. As one of ten siblings, my mother scrupulously managed her budget, making a habit of only purchasing the necessities. She often called us together to pray over a need as she faithfully led us in asking for God's provision. God owns *the cattle on a thousand hills* (Psalm 50:10 NKJV), she would say.

Continuing with diligence in our young marriage, my husband and I slowly paid down our debt. When we paid a bill in full, I'd zero out the line item in my notebook and scribble *Paid off!!* next to the expense. In some cases, I scripted *Praise the Lord!!* in black marker across the page. Being able to do that was so invigorating. I felt so blessed by God's goodness.

I've learned we can't go wrong by approaching each financial hardship with a Miracle Mindset. Although we don't always know how God will provide, the Bible teaches that we can have faith He will.

God will meet all your needs according to the riches of his glory in Christ Jesus (Philippians 4:19 NIV).

Not only have I learned of God's provision from the Bible, but I've also learned it from experience. Time after time, as we diligently sought God's provision, He answered with a miracle. Once when we needed a vehicle, God put it on a friend's heart to sell us his for the whopping price of $1. Whether it was a timely discount just when we needed it or a generous gift, God always went before us and made a way where there seemed to be no other.

Looking back, we marvel at God's faithfulness. But the real miracle we found in our financial woes was the boost in faith that came from our answered prayers. And we always stopped to thank Him—even for the tiniest answer. We praised God even when some said the provision was just a coincidence. And we praised Him even when the answer looked different than we'd expected or hoped.

Going to God with a grateful heart and trusting His provision, knowing that He wants to do a miracle in your finances, allows you to take your focus off your lack and place the spotlight on God's goodness. God *is able to do exceedingly abundantly above all that we ask* (Ephesians 3:20 NKJV).

The miracle of financial hardship is seeing God's perfect provision as we lean on Him alone.

When you can't seem to make ends meet, go to our heavenly Father. Ask Him expectantly to give you the wisdom to handle your circumstance even as He showers you with His perfect provision in His perfect timing. God desires to demonstrate how much He cares for you. He wants to bless you.

And as you seek financial guidance, recognize that the greatest miracle He may be procuring in and through the process is the faith He is blossoming inside your heart.

. . . .

Jane "Goldie" Winn

Jane "Goldie" Winn, MSS, has a Master's Degree in Social Work, is a Certified Life Coach, and serves as a client advocate at a pregnancy resource center in Palm Beach County, Florida. Having served in pregnancy resource ministry since 1997, Goldie's greatest passion is counseling abortion-determined women in the throes of making decisions about their unborn babies. She shares the story of her own traumatic second-trimester abortion, conveying that abortion is not the quick, easy fix often portrayed in our society.

As a best-selling author and seasoned inspirational speaker, Goldie has extensive experience speaking nationally and internationally on various topics born out of her own life story. Her book, *Rainbow in the Night: A Journey of Redemption,* was completed after 20 years of work and published in December 2019 on Amazon. Her story is now featured as a full-length narrative documentary movie, *Rainbow in the Night: The Miraculous Life Story of Jane "Goldie" Winn.*

Goldie and her soul mate Dave reside in Delray Beach, FL, and have been happily married since 1974.

She is available to speak, share her movie, and do book signings for churches, retreats, or special outreach events.

Goldie can be contacted at goldalah@icloud.com, janegoldiewinn.com, rainbowinthenightmovie.com or 215-990-7752.

A Bruised Reed He Will Not Break

by Jane "Goldie" Winn

I vividly remember my childhood home. We lived in a sprawling English Tudor up on a hill overlooking the Connecticut River in Holyoke, Massachusetts.

From the time my older sister was a little girl, my father hated her, abusing her both physically and mentally. The constant rejection my sister Esther experienced is beyond words. Because I saw and heard most of the abuse, I developed a real fear of my father.

My fear and anger eventually resulted in depression, and for most of my childhood, I wished that either I or my father would die. My mother used to say I was that little girl who carried a pocket full of tears wherever she went.

My father was a psychiatrist. In 1955, we moved to St. Petersburg, Florida, where he became the Assistant Administrator of the VA Hospital. Three years later, he was offered a prestigious position as the Superintendent of a large state mental health institute in Independence, Iowa, where at the time, there were 1100 patients and 500 employees. I vividly remember arriving for the first time at the formidable structure which was built in

1873. All the windows had bars on them, and the nurses were dressed in starchy white uniforms. It was easy to differentiate between the patients and the staff as the patients wore green gunny sack suits with "MHI"—Mental Health Institute—in large white letters on the back. Upon our arrival, my father exclaimed, "What have I gotten myself into? My first administrative decision will have to be the removal of all those ugly bars on the windows. This place feels inhumane, and that has got to change!"

My father was a visionary long before deinstitutionalization took place, which was the emptying out of many large state mental hospitals under President Reagan in the 1970s. Under my father's twenty-year tenure, the hospital was transformed from a custodial care center into one of the most comprehensive mental health treatment centers in the country, which, to his credit, is still open to this day.

As one can imagine, growing up in a state hospital made for quite an interesting childhood. Our home, the superintendent's lavish apartment, was located on the second floor of the main administration building. There were patient wards on either side of our living quarters, and often patients would get confused and end up in our kitchen.

One day shortly after we arrived at the hospital, my father reminded us to treat the patients with dignity. He exclaimed, "But for the grace of God, there go I." This set the stage for my lifelong interest in the helping profession.

The private persona of my father was very different from his public persona. He was deeply respected by the staff and colleagues all over the world. He was a sought-after speaker for psychiatric conferences and published many articles in psychiatric journals. Whenever he walked down the beautiful staircase from our apartment to the lobby area, the staff would stand to their feet as a sign of respect.

Behind the closed doors of our apartment, however, things were very different. My father's anger towards my older sister escalated with beatings and name-calling. She was a fighter and never let him win. She never cried in front of him but sadly cried herself to sleep alone in her room at night. I became more afraid of my father, as he had no respect for our privacy, and I never knew when he might suddenly burst into my room.

As a family, we regularly attended a conservative Jewish synagogue about 45 minutes away in another town. When I graduated from the weekly Torah classes, I was given the Holy Scriptures with my name engraved on the front cover as a gift. The Holy Scriptures consist of only the Old Testament, as the Jewish religion does not follow the teachings of Jesus and the New Testament. One night, my father burst into my room and saw me reading what he thought was the New Testament. Without giving me an opportunity to defend myself, he began punching me and yelling, "I will break every bone in your body if I ever see you reading the New Testament again." After the beating, his rage continued as he ripped the posters of all my favorite TV stars from my bedroom walls and stormed out, slamming the door as hard as he could.

My father never apologized or even listened when I tried to tell him he was mistaken. I felt hopeless and broken, like a bruised reed. I cried myself to sleep that night, wishing I was dead. Perhaps unconsciously, this is when I became curious about that forbidden book, the New Testament.

It wouldn't be long before my own rebellion surfaced. After that traumatic event, I retreated further into my safe and private fantasy world. I dared to hope that one day I could recover and find true peace and happiness. Could this bruised reed ever heal?

In 1967, I attended Drake University in Des Moines, Iowa, majoring in Music Education. This was during the hippie phase of sex, drugs, and rock

& roll. I was vulnerable and wanted nothing more than to be accepted by my peers. I became immersed in the hippie lifestyle, losing my virginity and experimenting with drugs, including hallucinogens. Eventually, I transferred to another college in Kalamazoo, Michigan, to study Music Therapy.

While my parents were paying for me to live in the girls' dorm, I also lived in a hippie commune, fully immersing myself in the lifestyle. I became more sexually promiscuous but never used birth control. It never occurred to me that I could ever get pregnant. I was truly living in my own fantasy world.

When I was twenty, I went to the doctor for a routine gynecological visit. To my horror, a series of blood tests revealed I was pregnant! When the nurse called me into the office with the news, I began swearing at her, telling her she was insane and that I could never be pregnant. I never used contraception but had convinced myself that somehow I was immune from pregnancy.

Reality took a while to sink in. By the time I came out of denial, I was well into my second trimester. I felt despondent and knew that if I told my parents, they would certainly disown me. Their acceptance meant too much, and I could not risk losing their love.

Sadly, I felt I had no choice: abortion seemed the only option to stop my growing fear. It was 1973—before Roe vs. Wade legalized abortion in the United States. There were no ultrasounds or pregnancy centers in those days, and when the doctor said there was just a blob of tissue, not a baby, growing in me, I believed him. To me, it was not a baby but a huge problem I just needed to get out of my life. Having an abortion seemed like the only way out of the crisis. And although I lived in Michigan, where abortion was illegal, I knew it was legal in California.

My hippie friends came to the rescue and sold some of their possessions to help pay for my trip to California and the ensuing abortion. In California, I was admitted to the hospital in my second trimester for what they called a *therapeutic* abortion. The doctor would inject a highly concentrated salt solution into the uterus, which would poison the fetus and cause it to die. Then medicine would be administered to induce labor to deliver the dead baby. I was told I would experience labor pains similar to a live birth. I remember the nurse telling me to press the call button when I felt the baby stop kicking. Interestingly, she used the word "baby" instead of "fetus," especially since the doctor told me it was just a blob of tissue.

The woman in the bed next to mine was also having an abortion. Even today, her screams ring in my ears, "My baby! My baby!"

By the time I pushed the baby out, I was quite numb, not allowing myself to experience any emotions. When the baby fell into the pan, the nurse blurted out, "Oh, you would have had a perfect baby boy."

At that moment, the psychological defense known as denial took over. I would suppress that memory for the next twenty-seven years—until I attended a Bible study for healing after abortion.

I left California quickly, needing to leave as soon as possible and return to school so no one would suspect anything was wrong. On the plane back to Michigan, I began to feel a lot of pain in my body.

As soon as I arrived home, I called a doctor. However, when I told him I was under the age of twenty-one and had had an abortion without my parent's permission, he refused to examine me. Remember, abortions were illegal in Michigan. He was unwilling to treat me in the event there were any complications.

My pain worsened, and I began taking illicit drugs to quell it. I gained weight and experienced flashbacks and nightmares. I had no idea I was suffering from the traumatic effects of abortion, today known as Post Abortion Trauma. I couldn't concentrate in school and began missing classes, which resulted in a failing grade in my performance instrument, the saxophone. Because I was a music major, this meant I would need to repeat the year. So, I made the decision to drop out of college. I knew my parents would eventually find out that I had failed, but at the time, I didn't know what else to do.

In a panic, I called my older sister, Esther, who was living with her husband in Connecticut. I told her I dropped out of school, and she insisted I come to stay with them. She assured me they would do whatever they could to get me the help I needed.

When I arrived, she saw how much physical pain I was experiencing and called the local hospital. When she told them I had an abortion and was under 21, they, too, refused to treat me, as abortion was also not legal in Connecticut.

Then, my sister insisted I call our parents and tell them what happened. I decided she was right. I had built a wall of protection around my heart to incubate myself from their certain rejection, and at that point, I figured I had nothing to lose. Scared and overcome with physical and emotional pain, I picked up the phone and dialed their number with trembling hands. I was astounded by the conversation that ensued.

"Daddy, I was pregnant and had an abortion."

"What did you say?" he yelled into the receiver. "You were pregnant and had an abortion? How could you shame our family? You might as well kill yourself. You are no longer of use to this family."

And he slammed the phone down.

At that moment, I was living my worst nightmare. My father had actually rejected me. He loved me conditionally—as long as I was a good girl and stayed out of trouble. This experience set the stage for my later spiritual epiphany, but at that moment, I was devastated. As I look back on that moment I can see the difference between the love of my earthly father and my heavenly Father. Though my father's love was conditional, I am truly amazed that when I accepted Jesus into my life all those years ago, I knew immediately that He loved me in spite of all my sins and totally forgave me without any conditions.

Minutes later, much to my surprise, the phone rang again. My father had a much softer and more compassionate tone. His words penetrated deep into my soul. "Janie, I love you. I am going to fly your mother out to Connecticut, and we will get you professional help. I will call the hospital right now and give them permission to examine you."

As soon as my father said, "I love you," all the pain in my body disappeared.

I understood then that the pain was psychosomatic, brought on by the fear my father would reject me if he knew about my chaotic hippie lifestyle culminating with an abortion.

My father made good on his promise and sent my mother to Connecticut to help me. After consulting with a renowned local psychiatrist, it was decided I would stay on the east coast, live with my favorite aunt and uncle, and undergo intensive psychotherapy.

The goal of the therapy was to help me claim my voice and talk to my father about my feelings. My epiphany was the realization that it was really okay for me to have my own feelings, no matter what my father thought. After a year of therapy, I was finally ready to meet with my father. I remember the moment I first saw him as though it were yesterday. With empowerment and courage, I was able to share my feelings from my adult self. From that day forward, our relationship improved, and I began to accept who I was apart from my father. I began to individuate.

In 1971, I met my soul mate, Dave. We were both coming out of the hippie lifestyle and in similar places developmentally. Our relationship blossomed, and after living together for three years, we both experienced a life transformation that would be the guiding force of our life together. Dave had been raised Catholic, and I was Jewish, but we had similar approaches to religion. God seemed distant and far away to both of us, and neither practiced our respective religious beliefs.

After we met someone who talked about having a personal relationship with Jesus, we were invited to a Catholic charismatic prayer meeting where people from many religious backgrounds were present. When we arrived at the ecumenical prayer meeting, there was a palpable sense of acceptance, unity, and love. We were drawn in by the love we felt in the room.

After a few meetings, we were invited to ask Jesus into our hearts as our personal Messiah and Lord. We gladly accepted the invitation as we were both searching for meaning in our lives. After praying the salvation prayer, I felt an immediate transformation. For the first time in my life, I experienced joy that could not be contained.

All the depression I had been living with for so many years lifted, and I knew I would never be the same from that moment on.

My life scripture came alive. *Therefore, if anyone is in Christ, the new creation has come: The old is gone, the new is here!* (2 Corinthians 5:17 NIV). I was given a prophetic word that I would receive the gift of joy. After I said the salvation prayer, I was flooded with tears of joy. A miraculous transformation had occurred, especially evident as I had been depressed all my life. I truly recognized that the joy I received was an amazing gift from the Lord. One I've never taken for granted to this day!

Another miracle happened moments later when I suddenly began speaking in Hebrew. I had never learned Hebrew and didn't know then that it was a sign from the Lord! The Jews require a sign (1 Corinthians 1:22 KJV). There was a nun present who understood Hebrew. She said I was praising the Lord for being my long-lost Messiah! It is very difficult for Jewish people to accept that Jesus is the Messiah since we have been told all our lives by the rabbis that He is yet to come and that Jesus was just a prophet. Whenever a Jewish person embraces Yeshua (Jesus) as their Jewish Messiah it is like life from the dead. I believe He makes His love so real that it is impossible to deny who He is. Another wondrous part of my redemption story.

Shortly thereafter, Dave and I decided it was not God-honoring to continue living together, and we set a date to get married. We exchanged our vows with God at the center of our marriage in 1974. We remain happily married to this day.

The Lord redeemed my life for a greater purpose. I believe what the enemy intended for evil, the Lord turned around for a greater good so that I could offer hope and encouragement to many (Genesis 50:20). To God be the glory!

This chapter was excerpted from *Rainbow in the Night: A Journey of Redemption* by Jane "Goldie" Winn, MSS. Copyright by Jane Goldie Winn, 2019.

FINDING THE MIRACLE IN FACING AN ENEMY

by Julie T. Jenkins

Facing an enemy is never fun.

Whether you are currently facing an enemy or have in the past, rising above the fray allows us to see God working even in our angst. Yes, God is a miracle-working God on many levels—even in and through our battles. Next time you face an enemy, set your mind on seeing God's miracles. Here are some you just might notice.

THE MIRACLE OF GOD'S PROTECTION.

God is omniscient—there is nothing He does not know. So, nothing surprises Him, and He is always prepared to fight for us.

I love how the Bible shows us who God is! In the Psalms alone, God's protection over His people is showcased repeatedly. *The Lord is my rock, my fortress and my deliverer; my God is my rock, in whom I take refuge, my shield and the horn of my salvation, my stronghold. I called to the Lord, who is worthy of praise, and I have been saved from my enemies.* (Psalm 18:2-3 NIV).

The righteous person may have many troubles, but the Lord delivers him from them all; he protects all his bones, not one of them will be broken (Psalm 34:19 NIV).

> *"Because he loves me," says the Lord, "I will rescue him; I will protect him, for he acknowledges my name. He will call on me, and I will answer him; I will be with him in trouble, I will deliver him and honor him"* (Psalm 91:14-15 NIV).

We can trust that when we face an enemy, God—our fortress, deliverer, rock, shield, horn of salvation, stronghold, deliverer, protector, and rescuer—has gone before us. He leads and guides us with wisdom and knowledge beyond our understanding.

THE MIRACLES OF GOD'S MERCY AND REDEMPTION.

When facing an adversary, perhaps mercy and redemption are the last miracles you search for. In the flesh, we tend to look out for ourselves. But God is love, and as we grow in our Christian walk and become more like Jesus, we will begin to see our enemies through a different lens—through the lens of God's love.

As you study God's Word and grow in His image, don't be surprised that the Holy Spirit plants a seed within you to care for those who stand against you. In Matthew 5:44, we are instructed to pray for our enemies. When we do, God does a miracle in us, softening our hearts to their plight.

As mature believers, we are able to praise God when He gives mercy to and redeems our enemies. And we also realize He continually does the same for us! We are all sinful; we all mess up—even in, or maybe especially in, our battles. Give God His due glory for the miracles of mercy and redemption He offers you and your enemy.

There is no one righteous, not even one (Romans 3:10 NIV).

For we ourselves also were sometimes foolish, disobedient, deceived, serving divers lusts and pleasures, living in malice and envy, hateful, and hating one another. But after that the kindness and love of God our Saviour toward man appeared, Not by works of righteousness which we have done, but according to his mercy he saved us, by the washing of regeneration, and renewing of the Holy Ghost; Which he shed on us abundantly through Jesus Christ our Saviour (Titus 3:3-6 KJV).

THE MIRACLE OF GOD'S JUDGMENT.

The devil is an enemy every Christian must stand against. Jesus, even in His perfection, had to stand against the devil's schemes and temptations.

But although the darkness sometimes seems to rule, we can hold fast to God's miracle of judgment.

In the end, God will win. Of that, we can be certain!

For the Lord is our judge, the Lord is our lawgiver, the Lord is our king; it is he who will save us (Isaiah 33:22 NIV).

We don't have to have the last word against our enemies: we can trust that God will have the last word.

When we are facing an enemy, we can stand strong in God's power, knowing that He, in all His wisdom and perfection, will guide and direct our every move and is in total control of the outcome.

"Listen to me, you who pursue righteousness and who seek the Lord... Listen to me, my people; hear me, my nation: Instruction will go out from me; my justice will become a light to the nations... Do not fear the reproach of mere mortals or be terrified by their insults... For I am the Lord your God, who stirs up the sea so that its waves roar—the Lord Almighty is his name. I have put my words in your mouth and covered you with the shadow of my hand—I who set the heavens in place, who laid the foundations of the earth, and who say to Zion, 'You are my people'" (Isaiah 51:1, 4, 7, 15-16 NIV).

DIANE LAWBAUGH

Born in Canada, Diane Lawbaugh met and married a handsome American who is still her favorite human after four-plus decades. She is a graduate of Westervelt College, a professional administrator, event planner, singer, and lover of all things purple.

Diane loves helping create transformational "aha" moments for others and has completed facilitator training modalities with Theotherapy, Sozo, and Heart Sync. In 2018 she became a professional teacher and coach, completing her Mastery and Certification training with PAX Programs Inc., investing over 1,300 hours in research, training, and teaching. Diane uses those skills to help men and women appreciate their differences.

In 2020, Diane published her first book *Connecting...the present to the past to find hope for your future.* It is available at Amazon as an eBook or paperback. She is currently writing her second book to help women and men dismantle misunderstandings and create better responses, results, and relationships.

Diane's ideas of fun are long walks, couch picnics with her husband, a good romantic comedy, and all things NFL—especially cheering for her Tennessee Titans. She finds joy in connecting people with hope, one another, and a better quality of life.

You can reach Diane at diane@hopewithoutlimits.com

BREATHING ON CHAOS

by Diane Lawbaugh

I didn't want to be in that room full of angry, disillusioned, and bitter women. I was 99 percent sure this two-day course was setting me up to fail at trying to fix our marriage of thirty seven years. Again. The problem was not that I didn't love my husband or he didn't love me. The problem was we were unintentionally hurting one another nearly every day without any idea how or why it was happening. My heart felt like it was being shredded daily. I needed the pain to stop. Looking around at other couples, I was approaching the conclusion that divorce was the only way to hurt less. That terrified me.

Sitting in that class, I was completely unaware that God had already started to breathe on my chaos to separate it and create order and beauty. That is who He is. The One who is able and intentionally conquers chaos. *Now the earth was chaos and waste, darkness was on the surface of the deep, and the Ruach Elohim—Spirit of God—was hovering upon the surface of the water* (Genesis 1:2 TLV).

God hovered over my chaos and breathed on it through my best friend, Deanne. She had attended a course about understanding men and women better several months earlier and repeatedly insisted I go. I'd definitely seen a positive change in her life. However, her circumstances were very different from mine. That was my excuse, anyway, to believe the course would not work for me.

My husband and I had a huge blow-up just days before my trip. I called to tell Deanne my situation was hopeless, and I was not going. I still remember the words she spoke to me, "Even if this is not the answer for you and your husband, think about the 1,800 men with whom you work." That hit home. This course was about a better quality of life, not only a better marriage. Internally, I kicked and screamed, but externally, I reluctantly promised to attend.

I listened to the instructor—stunned. For years, I had tried to justify my hurt feelings by judging my husband's misbehavior. Why was I convinced he was misbehaving? Because I knew a WOMAN would never act and respond as he did.

That was true and accurate. So what was the problem with my assessment? My husband is not a woman!

Since how a woman thinks, acts, and feels had been my baseline up to that point, I learned I needed a new reference point for my husband's behavior. I now laugh at the perspective that he was a big, hairy, and very misbehaving woman. However, until I recognized the lens through which I viewed him, there was enormous misunderstanding and pain in my life.

For decades, one of the most hurtful parts of our relationship was his constant refusal to attend inner healing classes with me. Living from the heart is truly a passion of mine, and it took me many years to clean out the pain I'd stuffed into the junk closet of my soul. I invited him often to join me in this quest, but his response was always the same, "No, thank you." Each time he turned me down, it felt like he was pushing me farther away. I could not reconcile how he could love me and not want to share my passion.

The instructor pointed out how two men can literally have a knockdown fight and then get up and go have a beer together. I immediately thought, *And how stupid is that?* But she explained that men can RESPECT one another WITHOUT AGREEING with one another.

In that moment, time stood still. That one difference between men and women permeated my thoughts. A mini-movie repeatedly played in my head. Despite having no interest in attending the classes himself, my husband had supported my pursuit of inner healing training. He never told me not to go and never begrudged the funds I spent on those classes. A sick feeling simmered in the pit of my stomach. *Wait. Instead of pushing me away, my husband had actually been RESPECTING me all those years?*

Had I misunderstood him all this time and judged him for something he hadn't done? Yikes! Could it be possible that misunderstanding my husband's motives was the actual source of my pain? That he was not the *problem to be fixed* after all?

This first *aha!* moment put me on a path I continue to walk—propelled by curiosity rather than judgment. Now, as I navigate each day, I ask three questions in all my interactions. These are invaluable tools, whether I am dealing with my husband, colleagues, family, friends, or strangers.

1) *What if no one is misbehaving?*

2) *What if we are misunderstanding one another?*

3) *What if there is a good reason for that?*

These questions help me see the person in front of me more clearly. When I give others the benefit of the doubt for their behavior and choose to be curious, I'm amazed by what I learn. With these tools and this perspective, the deeper connections I've longed for all my life have opened up.

Do I live this out perfectly? *No.* But God reassures me that my imperfections are not a problem for Him. *Remember this: sin will not conquer you, for God already has! You are not governed by law but by the reign of the grace of God* (Romans 6:14 TPT).

My life—your life—is governed by "the reign of the grace of God." He expresses His delight in you and me through His ongoing choice to extend favor to each of us rather than take offense at the sin that infiltrates our lives. God breathes grace into the chaos and messes of our lives. He is not put off by our junk. Instead, His goodness compels Him to act on our behalf. Recognizing this positions us to seek and receive His miracles.

Back to the class. God had more for me than learning to see my husband through a new lens. He breathed on my chaos to create a foundation of order and beauty in another way that weekend—by helping me see I had placed my hope in the wrong thing. I had put my hope in my ability to be pretty enough, desirable enough, and good enough to cause my husband to change and act as I thought he should. To act as a woman would.

Instead, I learned that my hope needed to be placed in God and how He created me. As God's children, we are already enough. *It is not good for the man to be alone, so I will create a companion for him, a perfectly suited partner* (Genesis 2:18 Voice).

Society and life had screamed at me that the differences between men and women were insurmountable obstacles. But God's Word tells me He made men and women as perfectly suited partners. Something needed to change for me to experience the reality of God's Word.

I discovered I'd been trying to hope something into existence that isn't possible this side of heaven: being the perfect woman. I'd been trying to be enough of everything for everyone. If I could somehow accomplish that, my marriage and my life would be great. No wonder my heart was sick. The enemy is so sly. He slips deception into our lives, making it look true, and then beats us up with our inability to live the lies.

What are the sources of those lies? Advertising tells women every day that they need {fill-in-the-blank} to be enough. Sometimes the lies come from our mothers, who just didn't know any better themselves. For instance, my mom taught me never to let anyone see my fears and faults. She taught me that no one would love me if they knew. At the same time, she taught me I must always be mindful of how I might be failing to be enough. Talk about a painful way to live. My mom was not a bad person; she was simply passing along what her mom had taught her. My mother believed she was helping me, equipping me.

I couldn't see the crippling deception until God breathed on my chaos and separated lies from truth and darkness from light.

In the darkness, I heard a condemning voice in my head telling me how much I was falling short. It continually taunted me with how I could never be enough. With that as my reality, any hope for our marriage seemed impossible.

I wasn't intentionally choosing to rely on my own capabilities rather than God's ability. But it took His truth to shatter the lies and set me free so I could receive what He had for me. For us. For our marriage.

God provided a litmus test from His Word to examine what I hear in my thoughts: *Long ago, even before he made the world, God chose us to be his very own through what Christ would do for us; he decided then to make us holy in his eyes, without a single fault—we who stand before him covered with his love* (Ephesians 1:4 TLB).

I wish I could tell you it was easy for me to complete the class as more and more *aha!* moments transpired over the weekend, but it was the opposite. I very much wanted what the instructor was conveying, but my past failures at fixing our marriage mocked me for thinking it would be different this time. In tears, I called my friend Deanne. "This is just too hard."

She replied adamantly, "You stay there and finish the course."

I did.

Shortly after that conversation, Heavenly Father reminded me of two things. First, on my 38th birthday, I had gone hang gliding and was lifted up to 2,200 feet by a power I could not see. Second, there was a time in my past when my only way forward was to trust God enough to step into the darkness of the unknown. He'd proven faithful to meet me and help me soar with revelations that changed my life forever—for the better.

Here I was again at the edge of all the light I knew. Would I trust Him again and step off? I made the decision. *Yes!*

I chose to leave behind the judgment of my husband's responses. I decided to listen to him with curiosity and learn what is important to him, what matters to him, and what he cares about. I would no longer see my husband as a big, hairy, and very misbehaving woman. I would learn to see my husband for the man he is.

The four-hour drive home was filled with a tormenting voice in my head, firing off doubt-filled questions. Had I made a huge mistake by committing to God the actions I would take?

In the midst of this chaos, God breathed once again. As I came over the top of a mountain, an incredibly beautiful sunset appeared. I heard Holy Spirit whisper, *If I put this much beauty into a sunset that lasts only a few moments, don't you think I have even more beauty to create in your life, your husband's life, and your marriage?* Peace settled over me.

To say I was shocked by my first interaction with my husband after the course is an understatement. I applied the very basics of what I'd learned about listening. Ask one question, then cover your mouth with imaginary duct tape and wait 30 seconds for him to respond. Don't interrupt. If he pauses, simply ask, "Anything else?" He'll tell you when he's finished.

When I first saw him, without thinking, I asked, "What filled your weekend?" Suddenly, a cartoon bubble with my question flashed in front of me. *Only one question at a time!* I counted the seconds in my head. (Thirty seconds is a very long time.) Just as I reached twenty-five, he started to speak. After twenty minutes, I thought he was finished.

"I guess that's everything that happened Friday night."

I was about to ask him another question when he continued. "But then on Saturday night..." He spoke for another twenty minutes to fully answer my question about his *weekend!!*

I was flabbergasted. A realization hit me: I'd been interrupting my husband for 37 years. No wonder he was frustrated with me so much of the time!!

I recognized I had much to learn about my husband and how often I'd misunderstood him. Not surprisingly, I needed to change to learn these things.

Please hear me when I say my choice to understand more about men—be it my husband, colleagues, family members, or friends—was driven by my desire for a better quality of life—for me. It was NOT driven by a desire to change *for them.* However, the outcome continues to be a win/win!

What a delightful discovery to grasp how much men admire women and are amazed by us. For years, I refused to ask for help or receive unsolicited assistance when offered by a man because I misunderstood his motive. I had believed the only reason a man helps a woman is that he thinks she is inept or incapable. Nothing could be further from the truth. Men want the opportunity to help women, especially women who are important to them, simply to make her quality of life better. When I was working in corporate America, I was surrounded by 1,800 individuals who wanted to help me. Allowing them to help me was a win for them and certainly a blessing to me!

On a more personal note, my previous viewpoint didn't allow me to understand how strongly my husband desired to make me happy and make my life better. Every day, he literally competes for me to choose him. How do I know that? A few years after my first course, I was studying for my certification to teach and coach this material. One day, while researching the subject of competition, I asked him, "How do you win during the day when we are interacting with one another?"

"Am I competing to make you laugh? YES!" He ardently continued, "Am I competing to make you like me, love me, want me, desire me? Absolutely. Because there is somebody else out there who might want to do the same, and you might look at them more than you look at me."

His answer took my breath away—41 years of marriage and still every day he competes for me to choose him. Curiosity, what I'd learned in the class, prompted me to ask that question. Conversations like this one continue to make our marriage a partnership where we choose to give each other the benefit of the doubt rather than jump to the conclusion that the other person is misbehaving. And instead of heading to divorce court, we have stayed together, recently celebrating our 46th wedding anniversary joyfully and with thanksgiving.

When God breathes on our chaos, bringing order and beauty, we are required to evolve rather than remain stagnant. His answers may not take the form you expect. However, experience has taught me not to limit or put qualifications on His answers. When I trust God, He provides beyond what I think is possible. Each time I trust His answer, regardless of its form, it becomes easier to follow His leading the next time. Over and over, I have tasted God's promise: *No one's ever seen or heard anything like this, never so much as imagined anything quite like it—What God has arranged for those who love him* (1 Corinthians 2:9 MSG).

In the midst of the chaos swirling in our marriage, I believed I knew the miracle God needed to provide: make me a perfect woman and fix my husband.

God knew better.

Color me very surprised by how God miraculously transformed me from being a woman who so desperately did not want to be in a class of angry, disillusioned, and bitter women to being a woman enthralled by men and the way God created them.

Living curiously in an effort to see, understand, and appreciate the distinctions between men and women added so much abundance to my life. Had I continued to judge my husband and all men as adversaries due to our differences, I would have missed many wonderful gifts that have come from our interactions. Now, whether with my husband, needing help from a stranger to reach the top shelf in a grocery store or emailing a colleague with a request, men continue to astound me with how quickly and consistently they want to protect and provide for the people in their lives.

It took courage and a miracle to leave behind my familiar mindset and live life differently. But God continually sources my courage via His faithfulness. Heavenly Father ALWAYS meets me when I come to the edge of all the light I know and choose to step off into the darkness of the unknown. I now know that's the best place I can be. I know I'm safe. Life shows me the miracle of God's mercy and grace await me. And it awaits you.

Our Lord is *the same yesterday, today, and forever* (Hebrews 13:8 NLT). He will provide the miracle you need, just as He did for me.

> *So why would I fear the future? For your goodness and love pursue me all the days of my life* (Psalm 23:6 TPT).

THE MIRACLE OF LOVE

by Julie T. Jenkins

In addition to all these things put on love, which is the perfect bond of unity (Colossians 3:14 NASB).

Love is the perfect bond of unity God offers all His children—what a miracle! This scripture, written by the Apostle Paul, comes as part of his instructions to the Colossians regarding the actions of Christ followers. His first overriding command is to *Set your minds on the things that are above, not on the things that are on earth* (Colossians 3:2 NASB). And then Paul puts forth a list of all those things we should be attentive to. Among other things, he teaches us to stay away from sexual immorality, evil desire, greed, anger, obscene speech, lies, and evil practices. And then he instructs us to lean into things like compassion, kindness, humility, gentleness, patience, forgiveness, peace, and thankfulness.

Now, that's a list! On the one hand, I love that Paul delineates how we can grow and allow God to work in us. But on the other hand, what an overwhelming task! How are we supposed to pay attention to ALL those things? And if we do, how in the world would we ever have time to address the necessities of living—like earning money, grocery shopping, and even answering emails—when we are so focused on all those other very important items on our to-do list written by Paul?

Enter the miracle of love.

Love is the sum of all goodness, wisdom, and perfection. Love is of God. God IS love.

> *Dear friends, let us love one another, for love comes from God. Everyone who loves has been born of God and knows God. Whoever does not love does not know God, because God is love* (1 John 4:7-8 NIV).

Love is the miraculous overarching call on our lives. Love not only creates the perfect bond of unity, but it will always guide us in the direction we are to go.

- When questioning whether or not we should do something, we can gauge the barometer by asking: Is it loving?

- When we are in the position of disciplining or correcting someone, we should navigate our words and actions by asking: Am I being loving?

- When we yearn to respond to an injustice, we can respond correctly by letting love guide our actions.

Love is truly the miracle answer to every problem or situation!

That being said, loving like Jesus is not always easy. In 1 Corinthians 13, we are given a description of love that, when taken seriously, can be a bit daunting. *Love is patient, love is kind. It does not envy, it does not boast, it is not proud. It does not dishonor others, it is not self-seeking, it is not easily angered, it keeps no record of wrongs. Love does not delight in evil but rejoices with the truth. It always protects, always trusts, always hopes, always perseveres* (1 Corinthians 13:4-7 NIV).

The miracle of love is that God IS all these things—because God IS love. So we can read those verses and exchange the word "God" for the word "love."

Let's try: *[God] is patient, [God] is kind. [God] does not envy, ... does not boast, ... is not proud. [God] does not dishonor others, ... is not self-seeking, ... is not easily angered, ... keeps no record of wrongs. [God] does not delight in evil but rejoices with the truth. [God] always protects, always trusts, always hopes, always perseveres* (1 Corinthians 13:4-7 NIV).

Wow! Doesn't that make you smile? Doesn't that make you feel protected and, well, loved?

And because you and I were made in God's image, WE are to love as God loves! So I ask, can you put your own name in place of the word "love" in these verses? That might be a little more difficult. But don't let it scare you, because God has promised us that when we hold to Him and follow Him in obedience, He will make us more and more like Him every day (Proverbs 3:5-6).

So how do we experience and exude perfect love that leads to unity? Day by day, as we come to know God more and follow Him in obedience, He will guide us into the miracle of love that cannot be fully explained this side of heaven.

Christ-follower, you will experience the miracle of *becoming* love!

· ·

DAWN VAZQUEZ

Dawn Vazquez is a former model who has over 13 years of experience in the development construction finance field, owns a photography business, and hosted a FB Live talk show, *Real Talk w/ Dawn*. She is also the founder of Women Empowering in Real Time, which speaks to and encourages women to revisit their faith, walk in His Word, and prove all things are possible and fixable through God. Dawn has also written for *Voice of Truth* magazine. She shares proceeds of her work with Women World Leaders for their women's global initiative, being the change she wishes to see in this world.

Dawn consults and speaks with women from multiple countries and even continents regarding health and business. She has appeared on podcasts and is sponsored by The Naked Warrior Recovery (formerly Navy Seals Fighting PSTD). And she thrives in her ministry work within her own community.

Dawn's hope for you is that after you learn of her story, you will have the courage to rewrite your own!

Recognizing God Winks to Develop a Miracle Mindset

by Dawn Vazquez

The path to developing a Miracle Mindset is one I have been on for many years. We all encounter challenges, but there's not a single challenge in our lives that God cannot overcome and shine His miracles through.

For the last ten years, I've been battling a terminal illness that tried, not once but twice, to end my life. The most recent time was June 17th, 2020. My mother received a phone call in Pennsylvania at 12:30 a.m. with instructions to catch the quickest flight out possible.

My body was sweating fiercely, while my inner core temperature dropped to 91°. I was experiencing hypothermia-like conditions as my organs essentially began shutting down. My body was completely out of homeostasis and unable to regulate itself or maintain a healthy temperature, a normal process known as allostasis. The origin of my diagnosis? Diffused, Systemic Scleroderma (a connective tissue disease) with Raynauds and mild interstitial lung disease—an insidious byproduct of a parasite I had contracted while deep-sea fishing.

I experienced violent fits of vomiting for what felt like days. I went in and out of consciousness, growing so tired. That's when I saw Him, ever so clearly. Not with long, stringy hair and an un-groomed beard, as He's often depicted.

I saw Jesus—with thick, almond-colored, wavy, shoulder-length hair, wearing a beautiful white robe and a golden rope for a belt.

"Lord, if it's my time, just please don't make it painful." Then as if using my one bargaining chip, I added, "But if I do make it out of this, I will dedicate the rest of my life to serving others. I'll make sure others don't suffer, and I promise to share my gifts."

By the single-handed miraculous touch of Jesus, I came through that fateful day.

The doctors and my specialist could never clearly explain that episode, or my previous one, both of which had nearly taken my life. They never had a clear answer as to why these episodes came on in the first place. And no one could assure me something similar would not occur again.

Looking back, God has been caring for my body, always supplying exactly what I needed. He had guided me to discover medical research and incorporate breathing practices, prayer, meditation, and different modalities over the years. His care and the collective results of the practices He gave me were what allowed me to live. It took me a couple of months to recover from this episode, but I was ok with that. How could I not be? God gave me the gift of life for the second time.

Six months after being released from the hospital, my first opportunity to serve Him—or God Wink as I call them—would appear. And it was not what you might expect.

I received a direct message through social media from a Polish designer I had previously modeled for and who now resided in the United States. The next thing I knew, I was at the Seminole Hard Rock Cafe in Hollywood, Florida, walking the runway for designer Naomi Besson wearing a stunning gown worth over $12,000.

Not a single woman there knew of my battle just six months earlier, and while I walked that runway at a mere 5'4" amidst gorgeous women in their 5'10" frames, I felt every bit as tall.

You see, I would now and forevermore look at life very differently. For the second time, I could truly appreciate how precious is the gift of life. Thanks to my Lord and Savior.

One year after being released from the hospital, I turned fifty years young. This is a birthday that I was told I would never see. I had been diagnosed one month and one day after my fortieth birthday and given a life expectancy of only two to five years. But God! We celebrated, surrounded by all things white, and, in true Latin-Irish fashion—with tons of food, dancing, song, and family who flew thousands of miles to share in this milestone. Cascading white satin swags hung from the ceiling, and glass votives adorned with white-blue feathers, shells, and crystals stood two feet tall! It was a birthday for the books! I set a place for Jesus at my table, if only in my heart.

I'm proud to say that the following year I hosted my first ever *Women Empowering in Real Time* event, where I shared my journey and various health routines, disciplines, prayers, and modalities I use to maintain a healthy lifestyle.

Due to the success of that event, I was asked to host another just two and half months later called the *Women's Empowerment Project*. I was determined to keep my word to God that I would be a spiritual warrior here in the physical, as long as He saw fit. As Proverbs 27:17 states, *Iron sharpens iron* (NIV).

Today, I've had the good fortune of working with women regarding health and businesses from multiple countries and even continents. I've appeared on podcasts, briefly hosted my own Facebook Live show, *Real Talk with Dawn,* and was even sponsored by The Naked Warrior Recovery—a group of former Navy Seals who have banded together to fight post-traumatic stress disorder. And, of course, I've ministered within my own community.

I presently continue collaborations in all areas of my life. And while it's still true that my health sometimes forces me to slow down or even stop projects altogether, I know this is not for me to question. With God in control of all I do, my job is simply to keep serving and creating as He guides me.

There is a much bigger mission at work here. If we allow God to orchestrate and direct our disciplines and practices, He will create miracles even among our perceived messes, illnesses, and chaotic terrain. He requires us first to open our hearts to Him and allow our spirits to be filled with His Word. I once thought that just going to church every Sunday would keep me close to God, but I quickly realized He had so much more for me. When I accepted Christ as my Savior, giving him complete control of every aspect of my life, His Spirit came to live inside me. Since that day, God has been walking out my journey with me! He's always there to help me, and He will always be there to help you, too. But you must willingly submit to His presence and invite Him into every corner of your life, graciously responding to His guidance and love.

Before my diagnosis at the age of forty, I struggled to understand the concept of self-love. I thought in terms of "self"—as in selfish. I was someone who attended church every Sunday, acquired homes, and made sure my 401(k) was intact. By outward appearances, I was doing everything right—living what I thought was God's way. So why, of all people, would God allow *ME* to get sick?

In my struggle, God granted me another God Wink. Those without a Miracle Mindset might say I was simply in the right place at the right time, but I know God's miracles when I see them. As I openly questioned my faith, I continued to attend church services. At one of these very services, I heard Pastor Todd Mullins of Christ Fellowship, Palm Beach, Gardens, Florida, speak about God only giving you what He knows you can handle. In that moment, I went from feeling like a victim to wanting to become a spiritual warrior. I chose to become the ambassador of this illness, avenging a death sentence that I personally saw other women lose their battle to just 24 months in. I wanted to give women a sense of hope. I wanted to show women who had never leaned on their faith for healing, perhaps because, like me, they were confused by the concept of self-love, that God was always there for them.

So let's talk about this thing called self-love. I thought self-love meant showing myself that I could acquire all the material wealth that would enable me to live an independent life, devoid of needing anything from anyone and never having to ask for help. But in truth, self-love is recognizing there's a world out there that is much bigger than you, yet loving and respecting yourself anyway because you are a child of God. Self-love empowers you to care so much about who God made you to be that you are willing to lean on the Word of God and act as a conduit of His Word as you walk in service to others—especially during difficult times.

In essence, we are all meant to become teachers of His Word through the example we put forth as we hold to God through life, especially in times of strife.

Knowledge is not power without action. Self-love is an action. Self-love is taking time to meditate on God's Word and letting it speak into our soul, making a difference in our daily actions. That is something I've practiced for the last decade.

It would take me three years to develop a routine of meditating on God's Word. Though being consistent in this practice may be difficult, it also assuredly comes with the biggest rewards; that I can promise you. I'm literally living proof. In the pages throughout the Bible, Jesus spent much of his time in meditation, speaking to His Father, our Father, and seeking His guidance.

> *One of those days Jesus went out to a mountainside to pray, and spent the night praying to God* (Luke 6:12 NIV).

> *Very early in the morning, while still dark, Jesus got up, left the house and went off to a solitary place, where he prayed* (Mark 1:35 NIV).

For me, meditating before the Lord is a combination of mindfulness, meditation, and intentional prayer; it is communicating with Him in His presence and being mindful of the creation He has provided for me. I close my eyes and envision a peaceful, tranquil beach, ocean waves crashing while sandpipers dance on the diamond-crushed sand. God's sun rays warm my face as a slight breeze wafts through my long, wispy hair. My imagination creates a beautiful backdrop. I count backward from fifty, finding space in my mind between contemplation and chaos. Once in that place of calm, I recite The Lord's Prayer (Luke 11:2-4) like a mantra over and over again until it is the very essence of my spirit. In that moment, nothing around me could bother me. This is my time at peace, with Jesus and God and the Holy

Spirit, rested and open to receive His guidance.

For your well-being, I encourage you to incorporate into your life discipline, a specific study of God's Word, and intentional conversations with Jesus. Go to your maker, in sickness and in health. Don't wait to become ill to start to heal.

I meditate anywhere from five minutes to an hour each day, and sometimes multiple times daily, depending on how burdened I feel. Never put a limit on your time with the Lord. It's not a race. These timestamps should be more of a how-to-begin template to start your meditation journey.

> *I keep my eyes always on the Lord. With him at my right hand, I will not be shaken* (Psalm 16:8 NIV).

> *I meditate on your precepts and consider your ways. I delight in your decrees: I will not neglect your word* (Psalm 119:15–16 NIV).

As I practice resting in God's presence, I know He will provide the guidance that is necessary to lead me to the next steps of my healing. Perhaps that next step could be a phone call from a random friend—saying they heard of a treatment being offered at a medical center and suggesting I call to inquire about what they offer or providing simple wisdom on how to treat my body.

Please understand, God likely won't send a letter in the mail with instructions. I know. I waited, and it never came. But He will provide His wisdom often in what I refer to as God Winks. He will speak directly to your spirit, through the people already in your life and the connections you make, and in His Word. He will give you encouragement, confirmation when you're on the right path, and discipline when you're headed in the wrong direction.

Sometimes God reminds me of how he continues to direct me:

- If I hadn't found the courage to hold an event to empower women....

- If hadn't dared to speak in front of women I didn't even know...

- If an attendee of my event hadn't bravely shared with me that God put it on her heart to lead me to Women World Leaders...

- Had I simply given up after no response on the second text sent to the founder of Women World Leaders...

...NONE OF THIS WOULD HAVE BEEN POSSIBLE.

I would not have published my story in a book that is being read literally around the world. That's God. It's His voice you hear, being recited in the words of my story.

God ENCOURAGES all of us by way of these alignments and synchronicities. All we need to do is have the COURAGE (found in the encouragement) to go for it!!

The number one question I've received over the last decade when someone has learned of my illness is, "How do you get through every single day knowing you've been given this diagnosis?"

"Get up, make your bed, brush your teeth, pray, and exercise," I replied simply.

As I worked with women all over the country and beyond, I began to realize that sharing this matter-of-fact answer with them wasn't resonating. They were looking for more. Worried about daily emotional triggers, they wanted me to share a prescription for a magic pill to catch the triggers before the triggers captured them. Many women have been incredibly shocked to learn that, despite all I was going through, I wasn't on a single daily prescription for illness-induced clinical depression. Instead, I learned to go deeper with the Lord, listening to that God-given intuition and taking inspired action.

When I was first diagnosed, a specialist wrote me not one but three prescriptions for depression medication. "Shouldn't I be depressed first? "I asked him.

"Oh, you will be." was his reply.

I didn't fill a single one of those prescriptions. Please understand, I'm not anti-medication. One of the daily medications truly saved my life. What I advocate for, though, is for people to do their research and also go to the Lord seeking His wisdom. Be aware of what you're putting into your body. At my diagnosis, I received fifteen prescriptions. Yes, fifteen in one visit. I never took all of those prescriptions, and still today, I only take one prescription, handling my health holistically through nutrition, exercise, and daily prayer and meditation. *Your Word is a lamp for my feet, a light on my path* (Psalm 119:105 NIV).

Wanting to address the concerns of these women, I thought long and hard. The most simplistic way I can explain my determination and focus despite my circumstances was to bring conscious awareness to the forefront of every situation, decision, or trigger I faced. For me, it came down to truly being aware of God's leading and His presence in every moment.

The power that lies within this awareness is the reality that none of us will live without suffering. Jesus warns us all. This is not about trying to run away from suffering. In fact, this is about running directly towards the suffering in order to allow God's guidance to get you through to the other side, to the light. Faith over fear!

For many people, it's not the large, obvious triggers that threaten to take us down. For many of us, the triggers come silently, almost to the point where we don't even realize they're happening until they've already happened. By that point, we've already reached a horrible emotional state, which makes the illness worse and pushes us further toward depression, and in truth, further from God: the slouching posture, slower speech, and brain fog.

We can combat the silent triggers by going to God daily. When we choose to trust God each day and keep our eyes set on the miracles He has already prepared for us, He grants us the power to live in a state of joy, which is, in fact, a choice. Read that last part again. Aloud! Having a miracle mindset offers joy and happiness, and it is our choice!

Living this way is a process that involves a lot of spiritual work, healing inner child wounds, and learning to be ok with where you are in life. EGO stands for Edging God Out. Although our ego may be more impressed with how many shoes are in our closet and how many homes we own, GOD is more impressed by our acts of service to others for the betterment of humanity and how much we yield to His leading. This is how we worship Him.

Talk to God like you would your best friend. Talk to Him on your walks, in the shower, and before you go to bed. Thank Him for solving your issues and problems. I promise you He's listening!

It is not lost on me that without the support of close family, such as my cousin, mentors of over twenty years, a mother and brother who would fly at a moment's notice, and a special someone who encouraged me to speak openly about my love for the Lord, this present-day story might have been written very differently for me. I truly am blessed.

The Miracle of Peace

by Kelley Rene

Albert Einstein is credited as saying, *Peace cannot be kept by force; it can only be achieved by understanding.* When I first read this statement, my mind immediately went to Jesus on the cross. He understood our need for a Savior and willingly gave His all. He understood this was the way for us to gain eternal life. He understood His Father's will.

Einstein's quote actually encapsulates the entirety of Jesus' existence.

He responded peacefully when rejected by his fellow Nazarenes in His hometown (Luke 4:16-30). Jesus calmly used the Word of God against Satan when being tempted in the wilderness (Matthew 4:1-11). He healed the soldier's ear and did not resist when the guards arrived in the garden to arrest Him. (Luke 22:49-51).

Jesus demonstrated true inner peace throughout His short life. A supernatural peace that came from His Father in Heaven. Jesus often went to be alone and pray, gleaning deep understanding from the One who knows all. Proverbs 3:13 says, *Blessed are those who find wisdom, those who gain understanding* (NIV). It is the understanding of God's ways, God's sovereignty, and God's faithfulness that births an inner peace deep within us to withstand the often turbulent and chaotic times of life.

The peace of God, which surpasses all understanding, will guard your hearts and minds (Philippians 4:7 NKJV). If you want peace like Jesus, go to your Heavenly Father. He will freely give it.

And whatever you ask in My name, that I will do, that the Father may be glorified in the Son. If you ask anything in My name, I will do it (John 14:13-14 NKJV). *Peace I leave you; my peace I give you* (John 14:27 NIV).

In my mind, the most beautiful picture of peace in the Bible is that of Jesus willingly surrendering His earthly body to be crucified. He undoubtedly understood what was about to happen when He prayed in the Garden of Gethsemane, *My Father, if it is possible, may this cup be taken from me. Yet not as I will, but as you will* (Matthew 26:39 NIV). Jesus was fully man and fully God. He knew the suffering He would endure on the cross. He understood the full extent of the sacrifice He was making for our sins. And He accepted His fate willingly.

Not My will, but Yours be done. In His moment of desperation, Jesus cried out to His Father.

Calling out to God and inviting Him into your storm will position you to experience supernatural peace. It will enable you to weather the storm. You may not be able to control your circumstances, but you can pray to the One who does. It simply requires a mindset to recognize your need for Him and a heart to allow Him to step into your mess. Isaiah 26:3-4 encourages us, *[He] will keep in perfect peace those whose minds are steadfast, because they trust in you. Trust in the Lord forever, for the Lord, the Lord himself, is the Rock eternal* (NIV). Take your eyes off your problems, and place them on God. He is able and willing to walk with you through them.

> *Now may the Lord of peace himself give you his peace at all times and in every situation. The Lord be with you all* (2 Thessalonians 3:16 NLT).

. . . .

SARAH BUSSARD

Sarah Bussard was born in West Palm Beach, Florida, and grew up in Canton, Ohio. After high school, she worked in retail until she had an opportunity to work her way up through the legal field. Sarah worked for a firm in Ohio as an office manager until she moved to Maryland for a short time.

Eventually, Sarah made her way back down to Florida and continued working as a legal assistant. During this time, she became heavily involved in the church and her relationship with Christ. Capitalizing on this newfound joy and her long-standing love of the ocean, God called Sarah to start her company, Through The Waves, a Christ-loving, sea-saving ocean brand. She began hosting beach clean-ups and selling t-shirts, from which she donated the profits—all to spread the word about Christ. Soon after, Sarah began a podcast allowing individuals the opportunity to share the waves they have experienced and proclaim how they overcame them with God. God's calling hasn't stopped there.

Sarah is currently pursuing her master's degree in psychology and Christian Counseling. Her long-term goal is to start her own Christian Counseling practice with Through The Waves to show people that, with God, you can get through anything!

THROUGH THE WAVES

By Sarah Bussard

Born in West Palm Beach, Florida, my family moved to Ohio when I was about five years old. Each year we traveled back to Florida to celebrate Christmas with extended family. Despite not living there, I felt like Florida was home and that I should have never left—something was calling me back. Our home was a Christian one. My parents ensured we were grounded in the church, but although I always believed in God, I never felt I needed Him. As a result, I went through most of my life doing as I pleased and relying on God only when it was convenient.

As a young child, I had many ambitions of what I wanted to do in life, but I was never really sure what direction I should go. Growing up wasn't super easy. I was a pretty shy kid and was bullied often. I went through periods where I struggled with my weight and trying to figure out who I was, leading me to rely on others for approval and happiness, something I desperately lacked. I was often judged for my appearance instead of who I actually was on the inside, making me feel like an outcast. An outsider. Abnormal compared to everyone else in the world.

As I got older, I slowly emerged from my shell. I played basketball and lost a lot of weight. With this newfound confidence, I started talking to boys and became interested in dating. At about fourteen years old, at the end of my eighth-grade year, I began talking on the phone to a boy I had met through my best friend. After a few months of phone conversations, I decided to meet him at the mall—without my parents' knowledge. I had a gut reaction the first moment I met him, thinking No, Sarah, what are you doing? *This isn't right. Your parents would be so disappointed. He is so much older than you.*

But I ignored it all.

My lack of self-love and respect for myself caused me to devalue myself and make a number of bad decisions. I continued seeing this new man in my life, and as time went on, I found out he was five years older than me. I lied to my parents and slowly morphed into someone I wasn't. Due to my insecurities and need for affection, I began to believe I was in love with this man who was not fully present, homeless, in and out of jail, and on drugs. Sex became a topic of our conversations. I never thought I'd actually entertain the thought at such a young age—my cousin and I had always joked about being forty-year-old virgins.

One night, I snuck out to a friend's house to meet this man I now felt beholden to for my self-worth. That night I let the influence of peer pressure get to me. I lost my virginity—outside, behind a random carwash.

This was not what I had pictured. This was not like in the movies. I felt like I had just been robbed of one of the most precious gifts. For some reason, I believed giving in and having sex with him would make me feel whole. In reality, I felt more broken. This would lead me further down the road of insecurity—not only with myself but in my future relationships with men.

Months went by, and I barely saw the man with whom I thought I was in love. He was in and out of jail, partying, doing drugs, and sleeping with other women. I was completely heartbroken.

One day, he sent me a letter from jail, and my dad found it. My parents learned his real name and who he really was. They told me I could never see him again, which completely shattered me inside. Little did I understand that had my parents not done this to protect me, I could have gone down a road of destruction.

Summer was coming to an end, and with my first love out of the picture, I had a brand new start ahead of me as I began my first year of high school. I was so excited to finally be free of that situation and just spend time with my best friend. I was not prepared for that year of high school to be one of the most challenging years of my life. I was around many more kids than in middle school, which opened many more avenues for me to get into trouble.

As I was finally free from my situation, my best friend and I began to hang out with a new group of kids. I was excited to have new friends and create new memories. But this group wanted nothing to do with me. So I was forced out—not only by those I had just met but also by my best friend. She had gotten caught up in drugs and the deception around her.

Hurt by the situation and just wanting to continue a relationship with my best friend, I began getting bullied. One girl specifically began to talk about me and threaten me.

Then, to make matters worse, I contracted mononucleosis and missed about a month of school. The sickness affected the vision in my left eye, but after multiple doctor's visits, my eye corrected itself. Finally, I was able to return to a regular school schedule.

Upon my return, the bullying continued. One day with all the pressures around me, I started a fight with the girl who had been harassing me. I walked right up to her in gym class and punched her. My actions felt like the best choice at the moment, but I would later realize violence was not the answer. I was suspended, causing me to miss even more school than I already had. By the grace of God, I passed that year, clearing me to move on to my sophomore year.

That summer, I met my high school boyfriend at the swimming pool down the street from my house, resulting in an eight-year relationship. For the rest of high school, I focused on him and imagined our blissful future together as a married couple.

Then, some out-of-the-ordinary things happened within my boyfriend's family, which led him to have trust issues towards me. As a result, he began trying to control everything I did and threatening me when something didn't go his way. I didn't realize I was living in a toxic relationship that was stopping me from being who I was and who Christ wanted me to be. Ignoring all the signs, we got engaged and started planning a wedding.

With meager faith, I began to pray, "God, is this the right relationship for me?"

God answered, giving me His peace, strength, and courage to end the eight-year relationship.

At that point, I started living just for myself. I had no intentions of turning to Christ. Although I finally felt free again, in reality, I was far from it. I craved immediate gratification. And having just ended a toxic relationship, I felt free to do what I wanted. So I began partying, meeting new friends, and caring only about having fun.

Stretching myself thin to please everyone else, I was utterly hollow inside.

Despite feeling like I was missing something, I continued to live for myself. Time went by, and I started dating again. I met another guy and fell madly in love. Again. A pattern had developed.

My new boyfriend and I were together for about a year when his employer asked him to relocate for work. I had a choice to make: Should I stay or should I go? I had a really great job, which made me hesitate. But I also knew I didn't want to stay in Ohio forever. So I decided to go.

The next thing I knew, I was living in Maryland with someone I barely knew. My job was different, and I was far away from my family. My first niece had just been born, and I missed her terribly. I was relying solely on my boyfriend for happiness. I had no friends, family, or faith. I was lost and a complete mess.

I cried every day, mentally drained and longing to go home. And yet I stayed. I had no idea why. After living with a near stranger and discovering things I didn't know, our relationship became even more toxic and abusive than my last.

I began applying for jobs in Florida, as that was where I always felt called to be. Having already quit my job in Ohio, I thought, *Why not?* Yet even though I took this step and my relationship was terrible, I still yearned for this abusive man to want me. I wanted his approval.

I did get a job in Florida, and my boyfriend helped me make the big move. It was the first day of my new job, and he was driving with me to work so he could borrow my car. Then, out of nowhere, things took another turn.

He hit me.

Completely in shock, I pulled the car over and said, "Get out!"

How had I allowed myself to get to this point?

After a few moments, he got back in my car. We sat in an awkward silence as he apologized.

I don't know why I stayed committed to him as our relationship continued to get worse. Thankfully, we lived over a thousand miles apart. Finally, one day, it happened. It was over. He dumped me.

I had put all my happiness into him and now felt completely empty—as though I had no reason to live. Hopeless, I knew I did not want to live my life as I had when I ended my previous relationship. I needed to do something different.

My cousin Amy invited me to church. I said, "You know what, I'll go."

So I went. And I completely broke down as I realized God was what I had been missing in my life.

As months went by, my broken heart started to heal. God put people and opportunities in my life to show me I was in the right place. God never takes away something without replacing it with something greater. My faith became so strong. For the first time in my life, God was able to use my mistakes to show me how much I needed Him. I was so thankful for the mustard seed of faith my parents had given me when they took me to church when I was young, all those years ago.

In my heart, I had always known that one day God would lead me back to South Florida. I knew God placed a love for the ocean and sharks in my heart for a reason. As a teenager, I had become hooked on sharks. The mystery of how misunderstood they truly are highly intrigued me. Over time, everyone I knew began to associate me with sharks. This was always the one place where I stayed true to who I was. It became my passion, along with my love for the ocean.

I prayed for direction. Now that I had a new faith, I wanted to share it with the world. Pastor Craig Groeschel had started a series at Life Church called the "Good Work." He said that by the end of the series, he wanted to help someone find God's direction for their life. I said, "Yes, this is what I need."

After the last sermon of the series, a few days went by, and I was still thinking of ideas on how I might fulfill my purpose and do God's "Good Work."

Then one day, it hit me! I was sitting at work, and it just came to me. "Christ carries us through the waves! *Through The Waves,* a Christ-based ocean brand." This would be a way for me to merge my two passions.

Since that day, I've prayed that God would continue to lead *Through The Waves* wherever He wants it to go. I am extremely grateful for all of His love and grace. He carried me through my waves to help me comfort others through theirs.

Philippians 4:13 says, *I can do all this through Him who gives me strength* (NIV). I know that through Christ, all things are possible, and He showed me just that. The same week God gave me this idea, my cousin purchased a massive T-shirt printer. So I began to create designs, sell t-shirts, and donate the profits. I also started hosting beach clean-ups to teach people how important the oceans are while spreading the love of Christ.

Shortly after that, I began getting involved with my church. I started leading a beach clean-up group and serving on the production team. I was serving God fully and wholeheartedly; nothing could distract me.

Then, it happened. The production team hung out quite frequently, and this guy kept dropping hints he wanted me to be his girlfriend. I pushed him away for a while, determined that nothing would distract me from God—not yet realizing he was from God. After a month went by, I agreed to be his girlfriend. *(I know, like high school, right?)* We dated for three months, were engaged for three months, and then married.

Our marriage, new and fresh, started so optimistic and pure. Until the day I found something from my husband's past that would lead me to begin to experience anxiety and panic attacks, beginning my season of therapy. For some reason, everything I thought I'd overcome from my past began to come up like a tidal wave of pain. Depression and anxiety swooped over me like nothing I'd ever experienced before. I found myself fighting to get back to who I was. Distracted and lost, I continued to press into God and His purpose for my life. I was seeking help any place I could get it: church, friends, therapist, inner healing.

A friend from church invited me to join her in a twelve-week freedom study to receive full freedom in Christ. Throughout the study, I struggled to show up and be fully involved. But I pushed through. Again, I was pushing through more waves. Then the conference came, and let me tell you, I experienced the Holy Spirit. He made it apparent that *Through The Waves* is His calling on my life. I may not be perfect, and I may still struggle, but I know I am free. This is something I now remind myself of every day. Who the Son sets free is free indeed (John 8:36)! I am free of any lie and any bondage that the enemy tries to hold me to, in Jesus' name!

The crazy thing is that throughout this journey of overcoming anxiety and depression, God showed me a new path. He showed me a path I never imagined for myself. I began to realize that because of the waves I had gone through, my eyes were open to an area of the world so desperate for God's guidance. God showed me— through prayer and various experiences—

that the next step for *Through The Waves* was for me to become a licensed psychologist and Christian counselor. With this degree, I could enlighten others and share the love of Christ with God's wisdom. Attaining this degree is a long-term goal and never something I imagined for my life, but at the end of the day, if what we are doing isn't for the kingdom of heaven, what are we doing?

In the meantime, through my podcasts, beach clean-ups, and whatever else God might throw my way, I continue to share my love of Christ and the ocean with others.

We are not meant to do life alone.

God doesn't want the waves of life to drown us.

God wants us to catch those waves so they can strengthen and empower us to help those around us. Through my waves, God has given me a Miracle Mindset to see His power in me. And with *Through The Waves,* I want also to help others develop a Miracle Mindset as they overcome tough life experiences through the power of Christ. The joy and love of Christ is always waiting to empower and guide us through the waves!

. . . .

THE MIRACLE OF NATURE
by Julie T. Jenkins

The vastness of the ocean, stretching as far as the eye can see with its blue-green brilliance.

The majesty of a mountain range, commanding the horizon.

The glory of the caterpillar, transformed into an exquisite butterfly.

The simplicity of a wildflower, sprinkled with the morning dew.

The miracles we see in nature are endless. And why wouldn't they be? Nature is God's creation, the canvas on which He painted and breathed life for us, His children, to enjoy. And God's majesty is endless.

In the beginning God created the heavens and the earth. Now the earth was formless and empty, darkness was over the surface of the deep, and the Spirit of God was hovering over the waters (Genesis 1:1 NIV).

In the beginning was the Word, and the Word was with God, and the Word was God. He was with God in the beginning. Through him all things were made; without him nothing was made that has been made. In him was life, and that life was the light of all mankind. The light shines in the darkness, and the darkness has not overcome it (John 1:1-5 NIV).

In his hand are the depths of the earth, and the mountain peaks belong to him. The sea is his, for he made it, and his hands formed the dry land (Psalm 95:4-5 NIV).

Isn't it miraculous to think that everything, all the magnificence around us, was at one time nothing but darkness?

I've always enjoyed nature. In fact, I kind of got a chip on my shoulder, thinking that it was all created for me. Because everywhere I've lived, God has given me a "favorite place" to see Him and His glory. As a child, I loved sitting in one particular tree that stood solidly in our front yard. That is where I would sing and talk to Jesus as I perched up in the branches, imagining no one else but God could see or hear me. In college, I had a favorite spot on campus that looked out over innumerable handsome trees presenting a foreground for the city's skyline that hovered behind. And as an adult, I've enjoyed the bike paths of Ohio, the hiking trails of Arkansas, and the endless beaches of Florida.

And, although I AM special to God, and I know that He DID make the miraculous brilliance of nature for ME, as a more mature Christian, I now realize that the splendor of His creation was always intended to meet each one of us wherever we go.

The greatest miracle of nature is that you simply can't escape it! Even in a concrete jungle, a blade of grass will remarkably peek through a crack, and birds will fly overhead, exhibiting freedom and joy.

God is ever-present. And so is His creation.

And what is truly miraculous is that nature, which is a *result* of the glory of God, *understands* the glory of God!

> *Job proclaimed God's greatness to his friends, saying:*
> *"But ask the animals, and they will teach you,*
> *or the birds in the sky, and they will tell you;*

or speak to the earth, and it will teach you,
 or let the fish in the sea inform you.
Which of all these does not know
 that the hand of the Lord has done this?
In his hand is the life of every creature
 and the breath of all mankind."
(Job 12:7-10 NIV)

And when the Pharisees told Jesus to quiet His crowd as they chanted, *"Blessed is the king who comes in the name of the Lord! Peace in heaven and glory in the highest!"* He replied, *"I tell you,…if they keep quiet, the stones will cry out"* (Luke 19:38, 40 NIV).

Yes! The miracles of nature are so vast, and they shout of the glory of God. And God created them all for you and me to enjoy. Let's praise our artistic and innovative Father, who, long before He breathed life into our lungs, envisioned, designed, and conceived an extravagant atmosphere where we can grow, serve, and relish in His love for us.

Let the heavens rejoice, let the earth be glad;
 let the sea resound, and all that is in it.
Let the fields be jubilant, and everything in them;
 let all the trees of the forest sing for joy.
(Psalm 96:11-12 NIV)

KELLY WILLIAMS HALE

Kelly Williams Hale is the Creative Director for Be Brave Design. She helps heart-centered entrepreneurs increase their visibility with stunning visual branding that captures and conveys their unique message.

As a coach and mentor, Kelly also teaches women how to cultivate confidence and find purpose beyond their pain. She's passionate about helping Christian women claim their calling and discover the destiny God has for them.

Kelly is also a sought-after speaker inspiring women to live their best lives. Her talks cover a wide range of topics, including personal growth, relationships, and leadership. Kelly is known for her ability to connect with audiences on a deep and meaningful level and for creating a safe and supportive space for women to share their stories and experiences.

She is happily married (third time's a charm!), a mom of three—all born about a decade apart— delivering her youngest when she was 44 years old. Kelly is living proof that past mistakes don't define future success.

Kelly loves sushi, music, and Taco Tuesdays. She can often be found singing and dancing to anything by the band *For King & Country*. You're invited to visit thebebravelife.com or bebravedesign.com for more information or email Kelly at thebebravelife@gmail.com

THE MIRACLE IN MISTAKES

By Kelly Williams Hale

When hope's dream seems to drag on and on, the delay can be depressing. But when at last your dream comes true, life's sweetness will satisfy your soul (Proverbs 13:12 TPT).

I recently had a conversation with my 25-year-old son, Dallas. He was calling to tell me about an opportunity he was considering. He's a sound engineer and has been working as a contractor for a company in Austin, Texas. A full-time employee was leaving soon, and the supervisor wanted to know if Dallas would be interested in filling that position.

As a mom, I'm thrilled that my adult children can talk to me about what's happening in their lives. It warms my heart to know they value my wisdom and seek my counsel. Making decisions at any age can be challenging, and having someone to leverage as a sounding board can be helpful.

Only this time, Dallas didn't want advice or my feedback. *Wait, what?* No, he just needed me to listen.

I must admit, I can quickly access "mom mode" when my kids begin sharing.

I tend to jump directly into *How can I help?* or *How can I fix this?* However, there are times when our children just need to verbally process what they are thinking and feeling—without interruption.

This was one of those times. And I was very proud of him when he said, "Mom, I don't need you to tell me what to do. I just wanted to let you know."

One of the most difficult parts of being a mom is listening without jumping in to tell our kids what to do—especially when we can see that they are about to make a mistake. Although I had some thoughts about Dallas's options, I had to bite my tongue! Years ago, when my daughter (Dallas's older sister) was 19 and dealing with life issues, a wise woman told me, "You are who you are, Kelly, because of the mistakes you made." That wise woman was MY mom. I wanted to protect my daughter back then, and I want to protect Dallas now. I have always wished my kids would learn from MY mistakes. Unfortunately, it doesn't always work that way.

My daughter was born when I was just shy of 20 years old. Having children was never a dream of mine. In fact, as the oldest of four, I didn't even want kids! But God blessed me with her, and then when she was almost 11, I gave birth to Dallas. And because God has a sense of humor, I had my third baby when I was 44. I like to tell people I have three "only" children.

When Christie was born, I had this knowing in my soul that she was not mine, but rather, the Lord's. I felt like she was on loan to me. My job was to love her, teach her, and guide her. And then let her go. This has been my experience with each of my children. But it's very difficult when they choose to travel a road filled with speed bumps, potholes, and winding turns.

We all will experience situations that leave us feeling hopeless. When our circumstances have stretched us to the max, we can feel like there is no way out.

We think that if God would just show up and fix things, everything would be ok. We try to avoid pain and heartache. On the flip side, we can tritely proclaim that God is in control but then do everything we think is necessary to help Him along.

But the Bible tells us,

> *My fellow believers, when it seems as though you are facing nothing but difficulties see it as an invaluable opportunity to experience the greatest joy that you can! For you know that when your faith is tested it stirs up power within you to endure all things. And then as your endurance grows even stronger it will release perfection into every part of your being until there is nothing missing and nothing lacking.*
>
> *And if anyone longs to be wise, ask God for wisdom and he will give it! He won't see your lack of wisdom as an opportunity to scold you over your failures but he will overwhelm your failures with his generous grace. Just make sure you ask empowered by confident faith without doubting that you will receive. For the ambivalent person believes one minute and doubts the next. Being undecided makes you become like the rough seas driven and tossed by the wind. You're up one minute and tossed down the next. When you are half-hearted and wavering, it leaves you unstable. Can you really expect to receive anything from the Lord when you're in that condition?* (James 1:2-8 TPT).

One of the most significant moments of hopelessness in my life occurred when I found myself struggling financially. I was a single mom; my daughter was seven years old at the time. We were living in an apartment, and I found myself unable to make ends meet. I had recently sold my paid-off Dodge Horizon to buy a co-worker's newer Nissan 280ZX.

Because of my credit situation—or lack thereof—my friend allowed me to make his car payments. Owner financing, basically. Before long, it became difficult to juggle the cost of living and make my car payments. And to be clear, my mom tried to tell me that buying the car wasn't the wisest decision! I needed a miracle.

As a result of my poor choices, I was faced with a decision that broke my heart yet seemed like the only answer. My daughter would live with her cousins for a few months while I crashed on my best friend's couch in her studio apartment.

I remember so clearly feeling broken and hopeless, berating myself for the position I put myself and my daughter in. To this day, I am extremely grateful to my sister-in-law and my friend for the sacrifices they both made to help us out. But it was hard. I paid the price (pardon the pun)—the consequences of choosing too many expenses on insufficient income.

What can we do when we find ourselves living in the chaos of our circumstances?

The me of today would say: *Turn your eyes to Jesus, Kelly. Trust in Him. He is a way-maker, miracle worker, and problem solver.* But the me from back then didn't quite grasp the width and depth of God's love. Ephesians 3: 17b-18 says, *And I pray that you, being rooted and established in love, may have power, together with all the Lord's holy people, to grasp how wide and long and high and deep is the love of Christ* (NIV).

I walked by sight—and things didn't look good—rather than faith. Yet looking back now, I can see clearly that the Lord used that experience in my life to strengthen me. Jesus was with me during all of it. The beauty of God's grace is that nothing is wasted. *And we know that in all things God works for the good of those who love him, who have been called according to his purpose* (Romans 8:28 NIV).

I would like to be able to say that when I got back on my feet, my life became roses and rainbows. But that wouldn't be true. It would take many more mistakes and bad decisions before I could understand how God takes our mess and creates a beautiful message.

My experiences have been my most valuable teachers. Their lessons are literally priceless, and honestly, I wouldn't change a thing. Today I am who I am because of the choices I made, just like my mom told me years ago.

Why do some of us go through the circumstances of life and remain relatively unscathed while others seem to repeat self-defeating patterns?

It begins with our thoughts, our minds. The Bible tells us to *take captive every thought to make it obedient to Christ* (2 Corinthians 10:5 NIV). But where do our thoughts come from in the first place? How we think and what we think about usually comes from our feelings and emotions.

When I felt like I was drowning financially, the emotions that came up were guilt, a sense of being overwhelmed, and fear. I felt scared and anxious with nowhere to turn. My resources were not only limited but pretty much non-existent.

My thoughts became a scrambled mess, which led me further down the path of hopelessness. I remember crying out to the Lord but felt like my situation was more of a punishment—I was getting exactly what I deserved. I remember thinking *You just had to have that car, didn't you?* And, *Why couldn't you just be happy with what you had?*

In other words, the enemy was reinforcing my beliefs about myself and my worth.

Much of our adult behavior stems from our childhood and the experiences we had growing up. Many times, we learn how to navigate life based on what we were taught in our family. Our beliefs about who we are and where we fit in are often introduced and reinforced by what we observe.

I grew up in chaos. Well, that's not completely accurate. My mom kept a beautiful home, and we had everything we needed: food, shelter, and love. We were a family of six by the time my parents were 27 years old. The same age I was when I moved into my girlfriend's studio apartment, and my daughter moved into her aunt and uncle's house.

I was the oldest sibling, with three active little brothers who kept my mom on her toes. My dad was a Vietnam War veteran; I can only imagine the horrors he saw serving in combat as a marine. My mom was raised in church and was very popular in school. She was a cheerleader and participated in many clubs and committees.

My dad swept my mom off her feet when they met, and they married right before he left for war. They were two young people raising a family without many tools and resources.

My dad drank. Looking back, I now know he was dealing with the trauma he experienced in Vietnam. Those emotions and the pressure of being responsible for a wife and four children were a lot. Our home life may not have looked chaotic to outsiders, but it often felt like it inside.

When my dad was hungover and grumpy, it was my responsibility to make sure my brothers didn't make too much noise. When my mom was overwhelmed or sad, it was my responsibility to do what I could to ease her burden.

So I grew up to be a people-pleaser. As a child, I just wanted everyone to be happy. As an adult, I never felt completely safe in my own skin. There was an uncertainty I felt inside, although it would be years before I understood why.

As a result of my insecurities, I made many decisions out of fear. *There is no fear in love. But perfect love drives out fear, because fear has to do with punishment. The one who fears is not made perfect in love* (1 John 4:18 NIV).

Through counseling, I began to recognize patterns in my thinking and behavior. I also discovered the truth in God's Word. I started devouring scripture and reading books from authors like Lysa Terkeurst, Carol Kent, and Sheila Walsh. When we believe—REALLY believe—who God says we are, our thoughts will reflect that truth.

There's a famous quote by Charles Swindoll that says, "Life is 10% what happens to you and 90% how you react to it."[1] I finally began to realize I was in control of my own reactions. As I was healing, I came to understand the impact of my feelings and the power of my thoughts, which informed my choices and behavior.

Our mind is such a powerful thing. We can literally cultivate a Miracle Mindset by choosing what we believe. The miracle, for me, was understanding that I was one hundred percent responsible for how I responded to my circumstances. I released any thoughts of feeling like a victim. I couldn't blame anyone else for the results of my choices.

A few years after the summer I spent apart from Christie, I got a job working as a production artist. The creative director I worked with was an amazing leader and was my first exposure to the power of mentorship. She instilled in me the desire to become a better designer.

I soon felt like I had outgrown my position and applied for an art director role at a local advertising agency. This was the next move in my career, and the pay was significantly higher. I was still struggling financially, so the salary increase was a huge factor in my decision. It took all the courage I could muster to submit my letter of resignation to my boss.

What happened next can only be described as a "But God" moment. My boss rejected my letter of resignation. She intuitively knew I would get bored working with just one client, which was typical of an ad agency. She not only guided me wisely, but she also advocated for a $12,000-a-year increase in my salary. Talk about feeling valued!

Words cannot accurately describe the presence of Jesus I felt driving home from work that day. I was on cloud nine and remember thinking, *I can't wait to get to heaven to tell Jesus thank you.* The miracle that day was marked by gratitude.

There are moments in our lives when Jesus makes Himself so known to us that our awareness of His presence shapes the direction of our lives.

Looking back over the past 20+ years, I have learned that leaning on God is always the answer to finding hope in the chaos. Believing I am uniquely and fearfully made (Psalm 139:14) and that God has a plan for me has given me a Miracle Mindset. *"For I know the plans I have for you,"* declares the Lord, *"plans to prosper you and not to harm you, plans to give you hope and a future"* (Jeremiah 29:11 NIV).

God uses our pain for a purpose. My experiences were all a part of God molding me. As a speaker and mentor, I can now show other women through my story that grace and forgiveness are available.

And they have conquered him by the blood of the Lamb and by the word of their testimony (Revelation 12:11 ESV).

The biggest miracle in my life has been the renewing of my mind (Romans 12:2). God has graciously transformed my self-talk from, *I am not enough* to, *I am a daughter of the King. And with Him, all things truly are possible* (Matthew 19:26).

The power of our words creates miracles. *The tongue has the power of life and death, and those who love it will eat its fruit* (Proverbs 18:21 NIV).

The enemy of our soul wants us to believe the lie that we're not enough and are unworthy. Satan would have us believe that the consequences we experience from making mistakes are punishment. The truth is that discipline comes from a Father who loves us.

Because the Lord disciplines those he loves, as a father the son he delights in (Proverbs 3:12 NIV). Discipline is meant to teach us how to act; how to behave.

No discipline is enjoyable while it is happening—it's painful! But afterward, there will be a peaceful harvest of right living for those who are trained in this way (Hebrews 12:11 NLT). *We are disciples of Jesus. As we follow His example while we're here on earth, our behavior and choices will bring glory to God. He will give eternal life to those who keep on doing good, seeking after the glory and honor and immortality that God offers* (Romans 2:7 NLT).

We all have a story. My children have their stories. What we experience—the good, the bad, and the ugly—is part of our story. Sometimes we make messy mistakes, but our life can be a beautiful mess when we remember God is with us. He allows us to go through storms, knowing we will sometimes make wrong choices, but He will guide us to a victory story on the other side. Then, we will have the experience to be able to provide hope to someone during their chaos. Having hope in all God is and is capable of is having faith. And faith is one of the greatest gifts that God gives us. *Faith shows the reality of what we hope for; it is the evidence of things we cannot see* (Hebrews 11:1 NLT).

By cultivating a Miracle Mindset, we can begin to handle circumstances with faith in God's power. We can learn to look to God, trusting His guidance to move us in the direction He calls. And as we grow, our example will become a message of hope to our family and the world, perhaps even changing the trajectory of future generations.

Rejoice in hope, be patient in tribulation, be constant in prayer (Romans 12:12 ESV).

In his kindness God called you to share in his eternal glory by means of Christ Jesus. So after you have suffered a little while, he will restore, support, and strengthen you, and he will place you on a firm foundation (1 Peter 5:10 NLT).

[1]Charles Swindoll, *Life Is 10% What Happens to You and 90% How You React,* (Nashville, TN: Thomas Nelson Books, 1992, 1994, 2023).

THE MIRACLE OF OBEDIENCE

by Kelley Rene

I have always been astounded by the biblical stories of Noah, Abraham, Shadrach, Meshach and Abednego, and Mary, the mother of Jesus. Their undeniable and unwavering obedience to God's commands is mind-blowing. In each case, the stakes were high, yet their faith gave them the absolute ability to walk out God's instructions in obedience.

In Genesis 6-9, God established a covenant with Noah, commanding him to build a boat. This was, to those around him, a seemingly ridiculous instruction. Yet, due to Noah's obedience, God saved the human race.

I've often pondered the complexity of Abraham's willingness to sacrifice his own son as God commanded him. When Abraham exhibited his intended obedience by extreme faith, God stepped in and provided a ram for the sacrifice and blessed Abraham and, through him, *all the nations of the earth* (Gen 22:18 ESV).

Shadrach, Meshach, and Abednego refused to bow to the golden image erected by King Nebuchadnezzar, instead willingly choosing to step into the fiery furnace so they could be obedient to God (Daniel 3). They trusted that He was in control of the outcome, and He delivered them.

I desire to emulate Mary's courageous obedience! When she was a young, unmarried virgin, the angel Gabriel visited her with the message that she would conceive and give birth to a son named Jesus who would *"be great and ...called the Son of the Most High"* (Luke 1:32 NIV) Mary responded obediently with her words, *"Let it be to me according to your word"* (Luke 1:38 NKJV).

Too often, fear overtakes my faithful obedience. Time after time, I question the inner voice directing me to step out. When compelled to give a message of encouragement or offer to pray for a stranger, I often hesitate. *They'll think I'm crazy,* is usually my first thought.

However, on the occasions when my heart aligns with God's, and I obey, I get a front-row seat to an exciting move of God, and my faith is bolstered.

Several years ago, I felt the overwhelming need to pray for a woman I barely knew. I mustered the boldness to ask her if I could pray for her. She excitedly accepted.

Okay, God, now I need You to give me the right words, I silently prayed.

I placed my hand on her arm and thanked God aloud for her. Thoughts of various details from our past conversations came to mind, and I asked God to minister to each one. I prayed for her daughter, who lived in another state, asking God to provide a way for her to visit. On and on, I prayed until nothing else came to mind. When I ended the prayer and opened my eyes, I was shocked to see tears streaming down her face.

"How did you know to pray for all that?" She asked.

"I just prayed what God put on my heart."

I have no doubt that God gave me the desire to pray for her and the very words to do so. She was overjoyed, and I felt overwhelmed by God's goodness to allow me to bless her. Some time later, the opportunity arose for her to move closer to her daughter. *What an incredible provision of God!*

Deuteronomy 28:9 proclaims, *The Lord will establish you as his holy people, as he promised you on oath, if you keep the commands of the Lord your God and walk in obedience to him* (NIV).

When we follow God's call obediently, we demonstrate our love for God. And then, we are blessed as we witness the activation of His miraculous power for all the world to see.

. . . .

Karen Burch

Karen Burch knows that Jesus is her number 1. She is married to her husband James, who writes and plays music, singing with a Motown-quality voice. One of his songs, Spoon Girl, is written about Karen.

Karen and James have two sons. Daniel raises chickens and has a fine rooster, a Great Pyrenees. Daniel and his exceptionally talented wife, Shelby, raise two of the kindest sons in the world. Daniel engineers sound systems for homes and businesses with KS Audio, and Shelby is in Church Ministry. Their son, Josh, is raising four of the most joyful and secure children on earth with his wife, Jenny. Josh is a structural engineer for Boeing; he also cooks, bakes, and engineers children's activities. Jenny homeschools their four children, is an avid gardener growing beautiful flowers and fruit, and helps women get the supplies and instruction they need for cooking and raising young ones.

Karen writes poems and songs about Jesus. Some of these are children's curriculum, like Reading Right. She is a best-selling author, having contributed to the book, *Victories: Claiming Freedom in Christ*. She also enjoyed writing *The Gospel Alphabet* with her husband, James, *Lamby the Lullaby Lamb, and Training Wheels Kids Songs*. https://www.youtube.com/watch?v=YWl9TUvvkis

PURPLE FLOWERS

By Karen Burch

Among all the women gathered there that night, the one with the crippled hands volunteered to make the homemade card for the mother of sick little Kimmy. She drew, with care, a picture of light purple flowers, all lying down, with a single bloom standing in the middle. The women gathered to pray for precious two-year-old Kimmy, some of whom prayed daily for three months during that treacherous winter.

There are mysteries for which God, our Creator, gives us understanding and some for which we must *seek* the meaning they hold. Still, others have their significance locked away only for God to know and for us to trust in His sovereignty.

Kimberly Bitsko, a calm little girl at two years of age, had long, flowing, brown curls, striking eyes, and heart-shaped lips. Her dad, Terry, fixed neighbors' cars and helped his father-in-law like a faithful son during his time off, and her mom, Diane, who is also my sister, spent her time with Kimmy and her family. So it's no wonder Kimmy loved serving others, often serving pretend "tea and crumpets."

On September 29, 2001, two weeks after the historic 9/11 attack, Diane discovered that Kimmy had a hard abdomen with visible blue veins. She whisked her to the emergency room. The diagnosis was neuroblastoma, a very aggressive cancer. It had already spread to her liver, and her doctor called the coming days "Kimmy's Marathon."

During a sermon in church, I listened intently to the pastor say, "God says, 'What you have been hoping for will soon come to pass if you stay in My way.'" It was a prophecy. I was hoping for Diane and Terry to experience Jesus. The church youth pastor prayed for Kimmy, then looked right at me and said, "Your part in this is to love Diane."

I felt so inadequate. All I knew to do was pray. All our close relatives prayed, and many friends prayed. I shared Kimmy's story with the middle schoolers where I worked as a teacher's assistant. Many of them made hand-drawn get-well cards for her.

One day, Kimmy's two Grandmas surprised me. It was rare for them to visit unannounced, but there Ann and Dee stood with uprooted, green plants in their hands. They informed me that the perfectly good plants had been thrown out on the street grass pile for disposal. "We thought you might like them." They smiled. We couldn't identify the plants, but I was touched by their joint concern for life and planted them outside in a planter box by the front door.

Kimmy loved to dance, but the effects of chemotherapy were hard on her that winter. Even still, on good days she would lead us all in the dance to the tunes of Kimmy's Uncle James' piano playing. She astounded me with her will to obey even when she knew it would result in pain. Little Kimmy had an IV central line inserted into her chest held by medical tape so strong I thought it would pull a piece of her skin with it when being removed for weekly cleanings.

"Kimmy, it's time to clean your dressing,"

"No! No!" she cried. Her hands were held away from her chest to complete the cleaning.

After some time following this weekly routine, when Diane would mention the cleaning phrase, Kimmy would still cry, but her strength and bravery took her to the couch. She climbed up and held her arms out as if on a personal cross. She cried through the painful process but stayed in that position until the cleaning was complete.

Jesus went through the pain on the cross to obey His Father. Kimmy was a picture of Jesus.

As Kimmy's Marathon continued, God spoke to our hearts.

One night, during his regular time of Bible study, my husband read Isaiah 38. He stopped and announced, "This is for Kimmy." King Hezekiah was very sick, and Isaiah prophesied the king would die. The king cried out to God, reminding Him how he'd served Him during his life. God heard the king's prayers and saw his tears. He sent Isaiah back to tell him God was granting King Hezekiah more time to live. Treatment was given, and the king lived.

Frances, a friend from our church study group, dreamed she was watching white, spiral cells trying to hold on to red blood cells. One by one, the white cells kept slipping off and were flushed down the drain. She awoke and knew the dream was about Kimmy's cancer.

The chemotherapy treatments shrunk the tumor small enough to remove it. On the day of her surgery, Kimmy was on the operating table for hours! One of the surgeons left the operating room to conference with Kimmy's parents. He revealed that every time they sewed up one part of her liver, another part broke open and bled. As a result, Kimmy received eighteen units of blood by the end of the surgery, a lot even for an adult. Additionally, some of the tumor was intertwined with the stem of her liver and couldn't be reached by scalpel.

Kimmy's intestines weren't working after the surgery. They were sensitive to being touched, and the surgeon had to move them often during the procedure. Kimmy swelled with fluid. The doctor told us they would know in 24 to 48 hours if she would be heading toward life or death.

I fasted and prayed, asking God to bring Kimmy toward life. Diane played heartfelt lullabies for Kimmy. Linda stayed in close communication with the nurses. Kimmy's grandpa kept all the relatives informed, and her grandma, Ann, wished she could be the one bearing Kimmy's cancer. Her grandma Dee remained far from home to be there with Kimmy.

Twenty-four hours later, the doctor felt Kimmy was going toward death.

The news left us shocked and silent. Daniel, our son, reached over and embraced his Aunt Diane. His high-reaching shoulders absorbed her tears, giving her face a hiding place of comfort, if there could have been any comfort. There was nothing to say in the conceivable face of losing the beauty and joy--inside and out—that was Kimmy.

Back at home, I wasn't satisfied that my fast was done, so I kept fasting from food in any form. I was headed out to pick Daniel up from high school but noticed I needed gas immediately. I knew the manager at the gas station but hadn't seen her there in years. She was excited and asked question after question about me and the family. Not wanting to be late, I responded with one-word answers, then, "My niece is dying." She made me promise to come back the next morning. When I came back, she showed me a collage of photos of her granddaughter. As a baby, her head was swollen to three times its normal size. The doctor told the family she would be brain-dead and bedridden if she lived. The woman told everyone to pray, and she told them each to tell two additional people to pray. Miraculously, the swelling of the baby's head went completely away overnight! The photos testified of her in the hospital with a normal-sized head. The collage also displayed her granddaughter in a wheelchair at five years old, smiling and participating in school.

"You tell everyone you know to pray," the manager instructed. This was the answer I had been looking for from my fast.

At the gas station and all the nearby stores, I hung up pictures of Kimmy with her story and a request for prayer. The next day a checker from a store told me families were laying their hands on Kimmy's picture and praying for her.

God continued to reveal Himself to us.

In the women's Bible study at the church, a homemade card was given to me for Diane—a drawing of purple flowers all lying down with one standing in the midst. God had given the woman with the crippled hands a verse, and the request to make a card was her call to express this. *Women received back their dead raised to life again* (from Hebrews 11:35 NKJV).

Our family read in our devotional how God led Moses to make the bitter water good to drink. It was the source of the verse, *"For I am the Lord who heals you"* (Exodus 15:26 NKJV). Later, as I reread an account of my aunt's healing from osteomyelitis as a child, I noticed that the same verse had been prophesied over her during a prayer meeting.

Desiring to have a whole church pray for Kimmy, on Sunday, I visited the church my sisters and I had attended as children. Pastor Riggs still preached there. He introduced me to the congregation and asked them to bow their heads in prayer for Kimmy's healing. At the end of the prayer, *"For I am the Lord who heals you"* was quoted. It was Exodus 15:26 again, for the third time. In the Bible, God sometimes speaks the same word three times. I knew I could call this a word of knowledge. *For to one is given by the Spirit the word of wisdom; to another the word of knowledge by the same Spirit* (1 Corinthians 12:8 KJV).

I knew Kimmy would be healed by Jesus alone.

It was now February, and many from churches all over were praying. But, despite the extraordinary effort the hospital staff had made to save her, doctors saw no hope of Kimmy living beyond two weeks, much less two months. Diane and Terry received instructions on how to keep Kimmy as comfortable as possible and took her home with only medications for pain relief.

The time had come to plan a memorial for their daughter, who was no longer eating or walking. A social worker came over to offer help finding a gravesite.

"No!" I wanted to shout. "Kimmy's Marathon isn't over yet!" But I remained silent.

I showed Diane the card from the women's Bible study. "God could still heal Kimmy." I held up the photos of the gas station manager's granddaughter. "This girl was taken off life support. She lived."

"These stories make me sad," Diane said, "Because God chose to heal other children but not mine."

That same week, the Bitsko family, Diane, Terry, and Kimmy, took a trip to the ocean. Kimmy had never seen the ocean before, and Diane, especially, wanted her to experience it.

Now, a miracle mindset is not only faith/believing. It also includes humility.

> *Behold, the LORD's hand is not shortened,*
> *That it cannot save;*
> *Nor His ear heavy,*
> *That it cannot hear.*
> *But your iniquities have separated you from your God;*
> *And your sins have hidden His face from you,*
> *So that He will not hear.*
> (Isaiah 59:1-2 NKJV)

During the week that Kimmy and her parents went to the ocean, James and I took our own trip to the ocean for our wedding anniversary. For years, I had harbored a grudge against James for not paying a debt we owed my dad and placed a stranglehold of fear on him to not spend any significant money on us. But on that trip, during an early morning talk with Jesus, He showed me my own unforgiving heart. And, despite the fact I had been considering quitting my job to help with Kimmy, God guided me to keep my job—to help pay our debt and offer relief for James and our family.

That day was our anniversary, and I suggested we buy James a sweatshirt he previously favored. It wasn't a big purchase by any means, but it was a token of my change of heart.

Is this not the fast that I have chosen:

> *To loose the bonds of wickedness,*
> *To undo the heavy burdens,*
> *To let the oppressed go free,*
> *And that you break every yoke?...*
> *Then your light shall break forth like the morning,*
> *Your healing shall spring forth speedily,*
> *And your righteousness shall go before you;*
> *The glory of the LORD shall be your rear guard.*
> (Isaiah 58:6, 8 NKJV)

As James and I traveled home, I journaled about this healing in our marriage. As I did, I noticed that when I took the first letter of my name and connected it to the last letters of James' nickname, Jim, it spells Kim, like Kimmy's name. I reflected on the gift God had given me when He reminded me of the time I sang *Jesus Loves Me* to Kimmy as I left the hospital one night, and He graciously told me, "That song is for you, too," Thank you, Jesus! *But thou, O LORD, art a shield for me; my glory, and the lifter up of mine head* (Psalm 3:3 KJV). Upon our arrival home, we walked toward the door and saw a very beautiful sight. The plants from Kimmy's grandmothers bloomed many light purple-colored flowers! Before we left, not one flower had shown itself. I didn't even know if the plants would bloom at all, and if they did, what color they would be.

Kimmy had come home from their visit to the ocean—alive and eating! She had begun to eat food while at the cabin and loved the ocean so much that when her father, Terry, who was holding her, turned toward shore to walk away from the waves, she kicked him to stay. As time went on, she had less and less pain, allowing her mom to wean her slowly from the pain medications.

Kimmy's doctor explained that the multiple units of blood she'd received during surgery must have *flushed* out many of the cancer cells the surgeon's scalpel had missed. Frances' dream before the surgery had foretold this phenomenon.

By Easter the following month, Kimmy had gained her full weight back. Her face became round where it had been just long. She hunted for eggs like she had life and a will to live again. She was redeemed—like the plants from the yard waste on the street—to bloom and laugh and have conversations with her parents! A prism of colors from a ray of sunshine presented itself in one of the photos of Kimmy. That rainbow reminds me that God kept His promise to give Kimmy more time to live.

It was Easter Sunday, Resurrection Day! Kimmy was resurrected in the way the card to Diane proclaimed: *Women received back their dead raised to life again* (Hebrews 11:35 NKJV).

A ray of sunlight filtered through
To make this photo a rainbow, it's true
For Kimmy had been starving and sick
Her body was as a little stick
Jesus had said she'd be washed clean
Then made her as before seen
Like King Hezekiah's health sublime
Little Kimmy was given more time
Cancer washed out with the blood
Like God uses His cleansing flood
To wash my sin so I can run
With joy again and know the Son

We knew God had given us more time with Kimmy, allowing her wholeness so she could enjoy life and giving us the blessed opportunity to know her better. She lived lively, running up and down stairs and playing at the park.

Kimmy and I explored food together. On the days she knew I was on my way over to the house, she'd run to the window to watch for my car. Once she saw it, she'd move the step stool next to the kitchen counter, climb the steps, and anxiously wait for me to get there, too. We sliced, crushed, and ate all kinds of fruits and vegetables. When it came to mincing the garlic, Kimmy tasted that too, then put half of the garlic clove in her mouth and swallowed it down like it was something sweet. Amazing! We sang songs, and I would tell a few stories. There was a lot of laughter in the kitchen on those days.

In September 2002, a year after her illness was first discovered and seven months after she came home from the ocean, revived, Kimmy's cancer returned. The extended family met at Terry and Diane's home to be with her. The cancer had grown so large it crowded her lungs. She labored to breathe. After an hour of coaching Kimmy to let go of her suffering, reassuring her that her mom and dad would be okay, Diane's sudden thought was *Jesus, would you just take her? She can't do this on her own.* At that moment, Kimmy breathed her last breath.

When she died, we had the benefit of knowing for certain her soul was with Jesus, and she would gain a heavenly body, never to be sick again.

For our citizenship is in heaven, from which we also eagerly wait for the Savior, the Lord Jesus Christ, who will transform our lowly body that it may be conformed to His glorious body, according to the working by which He is able even to subdue all things to Himself. (Philippians 3:20-21 NKJV).

Diane holds a special memory of Kimmy two weeks before she died. She got up and danced through every song in the church worship service, not minding at all that others were watching her with smiles. Kimmy just danced for joy to the music of the Lord!

The family fondly remembers that wherever Diane and Terry went with Kimmy, she would eventually utter one word, "Home."

Kimmy being gone was a bit of a puzzle for me, and sometime later, as I was waiting in line with a group of people, I was telling Kimmy's story along with the first prophecy. A gentleman listening reminded me that seven is God's number of completion.

God was at work in our lives, and He was bringing it to completion in the additional seven months He'd given Kimmy.

At a ceremony held at the hospital for families with children who died during the previous year, Diane was given an Athens Blue Rosemary plant in memory of Kimmy. As the original Olympic marathon finished in Athens, Greece, I knew the plant's name was no coincidence. The Spirit of God had awarded Kimmy the blue ribbon in her marathon of courage. Her race was one of Olympic-size importance.

As you reflect on Kimmy's story, I hope it encourages you to look beyond the end of each story in your life.

Having a Miracle Mindset is looking for God's love at work in our lives and in others' lives, no matter what we go through. *God is love* (from 1 John 4:8 NKJV) and *Love never fails* (from 1 Corinthians 13:8 NKJV).

Finding the Miracle
in Heartache

by Kelley Rene

We all experience heartache—and in the pain of the moment, it can be nearly impossible to imagine that anything miraculous could ever come from our pain. However, when we give our heartache to God, He will use it in a completely unexpected way—and even bring us healing in the process.

I remember the day like it was yesterday. Six-year-old Kelley stood in the living room amidst the normal crazy of a young family. A hungry baby cried. My older brother and sister fought. And standing at the dining room table, my mother was rattling off instructions when the old-fashioned ring of the olive-tinted telephone affixed to the wall interrupted the drum of her voice. My dad held the receiver out to her, and she swiped it up to her ear.

The message she received that day sent her into a frenzy, opening a crevasse of heartache. She would never be the same. With an ear-piercing scream, she dropped to the floor and began to sob.

Her mother had been brutally murdered in the early hours of the morning.

Even as a little girl, I recognized her agony. Her heartache got hung up on questions she grappled with, questions for which she had no answers. *How could this happen? Why her mother? Why had she neglected her after their last argument?*

She cried. She prayed. And eventually, she gave it to God. There was nothing she could do to bring her mother back. Psalm 34:18 says *The Lord is close to the brokenhearted; he rescues those whose spirits are crushed* (NLT). A devout Christian, my mother knew her heavenly Father had endured excruciating pain when His Son went to the cross and now understood hers. God could and did soothe her agonizing sorrow when she finally released it to Him.

Over the years, her heartache slowly morphed into a miracle as she learned to use her grief as a catapult to serve others. She made time for friends who had lost loved ones—grieving with them, praying with them, and encouraging them to seek comfort in the arms of the only One who could truly heal their hearts. She understood their pain as many could not. God turned her heartache into a miracle that allowed her to minister to those around her who were hurting and wounded.

God restores those whose hearts are crushed. *"He will wipe every tear from their eyes, and there will be no more death or sorrow or crying or pain. All these things are gone forever."* And from His throne, He said, *"Look, I'm making everything new!"* (Rev 21:4, 5 NLT)

Jesus tells us in John 16:33, *"I have told you all this so that you may have peace in me. Here on earth you will have many trials and sorrows. But take heart, because I have overcome the world"* (NLT).

When you experience heartache, give your pain to the One who understands and desires to wipe away every tear. Jesus is willing and able to mend your broken heart, and He will turn your brokenness into a miracle that ministers to others in their time of need.

. . . .

AFTERWORD

As Having a Miracle Mindset means focusing our eyes and hearts on Jesus and His wonders. It is living with total abandon and sold-out trust to the One who loves you more than you can imagine.

Our God is a miracle worker who never hesitates to step into our chaos. With His sovereign authority over all creation, He alone can miraculously turn our wreckage into restoration, our turmoil into triumph, and our mayhem into majesty.

Only Jesus can offer us perfection. And by believing in our hearts and stating with our words that He is the truth, the way, and the life, we are granted the greatest miracle of all—eternity with God our Father in heaven.

As we walk this earth, we are given the opportunity to live with a Miracle Mindset by choosing an activated faith that trusts beyond a shadow of a doubt that God is sovereign. He remains in control even when circumstances seem out of control. He's always watching, always protecting, and always directing us. Even when life makes absolutely no sense, we can remain focused on Him with a heart of gratitude, knowing He is faithful to lead us in the perfect path.

Philippians 4:6-7 reminds us, *Don't worry about anything; instead, pray about everything. Tell God what you need, and thank him for all he has done.*

Then you will experience God's peace, which exceeds anything we can understand. His peace will guard your hearts and minds as you live in Christ Jesus (NLT).

God is waiting to step into your circumstances and bring hope from the chaos. When you allow Him to, you will one day look back and give thanks for all He did in your life. *My soul, wait silently for God alone, for my expectation is from Him. He only is my rock and my salvation; He is my defense; I shall not be moved. In God is my salvation and my glory; the rock of my strength, and my refuge, is in God. Trust in Him at all times, you people; Pour out your heart before Him; God is a refuge for us* (Psalm 62:5-8 NKJV).

A Miracle Mindset is living with great expectations for everything God wants to do in your life. Regardless of what might come against you, God is able. In 2 Corinthians 4:8-9, the apostle Paul sympathizes with our chaos and encourages us, *We are pressed on every side by troubles, but we are not crushed. We are perplexed, but not driven to despair. We are hunted down, but never abandoned by God. We get knocked down, but we are not destroyed* (NLT).

God is ever-present. He walks beside us, guiding and protecting us. And He stands ready to reveal Himself. We only need to stop, listen, and seek His miracles.

We can rejoice, too, when we run into problems and trials, for we know that they help us develop endurance. And endurance develops strength of character, and character strengthens our confident hope of salvation. And this hope will not lead to disappointment. For we know how dearly God loves us, because he has given us the Holy Spirit to fill our hearts with his love (Romans 5:3-5 NLT).

Our prayer is that as you have read these stories and teachings, you have allowed God to help you develop a Miracle Mindset. If you are still struggling in this area, ask God to help you focus on Him, the One who holds you firmly in the palm of His hands. Take time to be still, setting your mind on the fact that God is God—ever present, in complete control, and full of love for you. Ask Him to help you find hope in your chaos and give you a submissive heart so you might fully confess that He is trustworthy and always faithful.

> *"I am leaving you with a gift—peace of mind and heart. And the peace I give is a gift the world cannot give. So don't be troubled or afraid"* (John 14:27 NLT).

Keep your eyes on God, the author and finisher of your faith. And know that He is at work, making all things new and instilling you with hope even in the chaos as you boldly adopt a Miracle Mindset.

More from WPP!

World Publishing and Productions was birthed in obedience to God's call. Our mission is to empower writers to walk in their God-given purpose as they share their God story with the world. We offer one-on-one coaching and a complete publishing experience. To find out more about how we can help you become a published author or to purchase books written to share God's glory, please visit: www.worldpublishingandproductions.com

With *Joy Unspeakable: Regardless of Your Circumstances,* you will learn how joy and sorrow can dance together during adversity. The words in this book will encourage, inspire, motivate, and give you hope, joy, and peace.

Surrendered: Yielded With Purpose will help you recognize with awe that surrendering to God is far more effective than striving alone. When we let go of our own attempts to earn God's favor and rely on Jesus Christ, we receive a deeper intimacy with Him and a greater power to serve Him.

United Men of Honor: Overcoming Adversity Through Faith will help you armor up, become fit to fight, and move forward with what it takes to be an honorable leader. Over twenty authors in this book share their accounts of God's provision, care, and power as they proclaim His Word.

Embrace the Journey: Your Path to Spiritual Growth will strengthen and empower you to step boldly in faith. These stories, along with expertly placed expositional teachings will remind you that no matter what we encounter, we can always look to God, trusting HIS provision, strength, and direction.

Victories: Claiming Freedom in Christ presents expository teaching coupled with individual stories that testify to battles conquered victoriously through the power of Jesus Christ. The words in this book will motivate and inspire you and give you hope as God awakens you to your victory!